**JUSTICE
MY WAY**

To: Papa Smith
From: Marty

Thank you so much
for all your encouragement
over the years. I hope
this project brings you joy.

Sincerely,

JUSTICE MY WAY

MEMOIRS OF A BLACK PROSECUTOR

MARTINIS M. JACKSON

CONTENTS

PREFACE

At some point in our relationship, my wife and I were sharing our life journeys over dinner when she raised for the first time the idea of me writing a book to share my time as a prosecutor. I didn't pay the thought much attention initially but her persistence throughout our relationship on the subject prompted me, after many years, to put the first sentence on paper. After years of effort, her vision came to fruition. Without her encouragement and support throughout my time serving as an Assistant U.S. Attorney, none of this would have been possible.

This book describes my experience serving as an African-American prosecutor in the U.S. criminal justice system. It is a memoir inspired by my desire to share a different perspective on the system—one viewed through the unique lens of a black man. It explores the rampant ironies and cognitive dissonance inherent in my serving as an agent of a system designed to destroy people who look and grew up like me.

The book is divided into four parts, each concept describing a recurring theme that I discovered throughout my time serving as a prosecutor. The parts—empathy, justice, war, and purpose—are concepts that I believe any aspiring or acting prosecutor should consider before stepping into a courtroom and carrying out his or her duties. Each unit includes descriptions of cases that I prosecuted as well as my own life experiences, which support this proposition. The cases, though based on true events, have been modified to protect the identities of those involved.

By sharing how my own life story shaped my experience as a prosecutor, I hope to highlight the important role diverse prosecutors play in the criminal justice system—a system that should be designed to treat victims and defendants fairly. Additionally, I hope this book helps my audience consider the political and practical barriers prosecutors face every day in administering justice.

INTRODUCTION
You don't know what you don't know

The range of possibilities for humans on earth is only limited by their imaginations. As children, we enter the world with no concept of boundaries or restrictions. As our bodies and brains develop, we attempt to explore the world and soon discover that it has confines. We realize that there are things that we can and cannot do, or at least should not do. Many of these barriers are conveyed verbally by parents, teachers, books and television. Some are realized through experiences such as jumping from a playground slide or running into a brick wall. However, I believe that nothing has a greater impact on establishing the gamut of conceivability at a young age than the role model.

At the early stages of life, like most, my role models were the adults who raised me. As I entered grade school, my views continued to evolve. The only professionals I encountered were my teachers. My household was largely comprised of blue collar workers who had never gone to college. They rarely spoke about their jobs and when they did it was typically with contempt. Growing up, I never held a conversation with a lawyer, architect, or engineer. Although I had heard about them in school and on television, their professions were as foreign to me as Pluto or Jupiter. School work did little to connect theory to practice, which created a chasm between what I learned in class and my understanding about how I might use that information in the real world. I had, however, met a few professional basketball players in my life at basketball camps and neighborhood pick-up games. I understood their craft and witnessed the fruits of their labor manifested by women, cars,

1

nice clothes and admiration. In fact, some of my fondest memories as a child came while watching the Memphis Tigers basketball team with my father and uncles on the wooden enclosed T.V. in our basement and listening to them debate about the games before bed. We cheered on the team while debating coaching decisions and evaluating player's performances. I cherished the male bonding. I slept soundly when our team won and often cried in my bed when our team lost.

Like most kids, I wanted respect and love from my peer group, and the culture I grew up in made it clear that excelling at sports was an easy way to gain both. My family often stressed the importance of getting a "good education" and going to college. However, as a teenager it was difficult to connect school work with a tangible future result, especially without examples at home or in the community to explain what being a professional meant. I admired my family's work ethic, but I knew most of them hated their jobs-a path I was hesitant to follow. To make matters worse, high school peer pressure did very little to encourage excelling in school. In fact, I felt as if there was an inverse relationship between obtaining good grades and popularity, so even though my family demanded I maintain good grades, I only did just enough to avoid their ridicule. My true focus was basketball, which presented a few problems: I was 5'6 and 160 lbs. in middle school and had never played organized basketball beyond the YMCA. It should have come as no surprise that I failed to make my middle school team each year I tried out, and I was starting to give up on my dreams.

My first year of high school my family moved to a home located in a different school district. I was not happy about leaving my friends behind, but the transition offered me an opportunity to try-out for a different team. My father supported my hoop dreams, though I doubt he was confident about seeing their fruition. The first day of school my father and I sought out the head coach and asked him what it would take for me to join the team. The coach spoke briefly with my father and eventually invited me to pre-season conditioning. When I arrived for the first day of workouts, there were dozens of kids gathered on the baseball field awaiting the head coach's instructions with the same hopes of making the team. The group was comprised of all ages, sizes and experience levels. Eventually, the coach strolled out onto the field and explained that we had to run three miles around the baseball field to begin our training. After a brief speech describing our task, he walked fifty yards into the distance and stood under the shade where he would watch us run. Once he turned his back to leave, the seniors took over the speech where the coach left off.

"If you get lapped, you might as well take your ass home!" one senior said.

At that point, the running began. I was a horrible basketball player and it was evident to others without ever having watched me play. With just one look at the pink jogging pants and white t-shirt I wore over my boney frame during conditioning, it was clear that I was no Allen Iverson, but I could do one thing that others on the field that day could not: endure pain. After the first day of running, members of the group started falling like dominoes, some of them walked off the field before finishing the three miles, never to be seen again. Once we completed our workout, the coach marched back over to the group to inform us that conditioning started in August and ended in November. The idea of running three miles a day and then going into the gym to run additional sprints for four months straight deterred many of the prospective players. Each day fewer and fewer people showed up, until one day it was just me and the upperclassmen who were virtually already on the team. I never missed a day of running, even when I was sick or it rained. After workouts we would play pick-up games at the nearby middle school gym, since the high school gym was being renovated. The upperclassmen were bigger, faster, and stronger than I was, and they exploited my presence on the court at every turn. The games were extremely competitive, and I was often berated for my lack of skill, but, in time, they came to accept my inexperience and their ridicule turned into teaching. Running, however, I could do, and the seniors cut me no slack on that task.

Initially, the seniors would lap me after a few miles and heckle me as they passed by.

"Fresh meat, pick it up!" they said.

After a month of running, I was still in last place, but no one was lapping me. After two months, I was staying with the group but not passing anyone out of fear of showing off.

When November came around and tryouts were held, many of the prospects who gave up on pre-season conditioning re-emerged. Most of them were more skilled than I was and had experience playing in middle school or AAU. The day of tryouts I was prepared to do whatever it took to make the team; I would dive on the floor for loose balls, rebound, and play defense like a man possessed if I needed to. The coach walked into the newly renovated gym and saw two groups of young men: one group sitting high up in the bleachers comprised of the seniors and upperclassmen from conditioning who were already on the team and the other group filled with prospects who would need to tryout, including myself. When the coach passed the prospect group, he noticed me sitting among them and signaled to me that I should walk with him. Shocked, I got up and trailed him as he walked over to the seniors and underclassmen. When he told me to sit with the team, I felt a feeling that I had never experienced before. It was the first time in my life that I felt like I was a part of something that I had earned. I had given my all and reaped the rewards of my labor. At that moment, the coach had taught me a lesson that resonated with me my entire life: skill is important but sometimes resilience is equally important. Basketball became my first love. I spent all my time thinking about it and working to get better at it. If I wasn't outside practicing my ball handling, I was lying on my bed working on my shooting form. I became a student of high school, college, and NBA basketball. I spent hours analyzing games and practicing moves. Everything else in life became secondary.

My first year on the team, I saw very little action. Honestly, I spent most of my time as the varsity team's water and camera boy. I was tasked with hauling the towels and Gatorade to each varsity game and then running the camera for post-game analysis. I was the target of laughter by my peers daily. I recall roundtable discussions where teammates would randomly ask others at the table who the "sorriest" player on the team was and many fingers pointed to me. Some of the players would avoid answering out of pity, others would take pride in simply knowing that it wasn't them. I learned to endure criticism and stand alone when no one else defended me. Plus, being the water and camera boy did have some advantages: I traveled to the varsity team's games throughout the year. During my freshman year, our varsity team was one of the best in the city. That was saying a lot in Memphis, a city that produced a collection of professional basketball players and continued to house some of the nation's top prospects. I gained early exposure to some of the most talented high school basketball players in the region. I saw how fast, strong and smart the players were. I listened to half-time speeches and picked up on jargon. I saw what it took to win. As water boy, I also attended varsity practice. During practice, I saw the importance of senior leadership and accountability. The seniors worked the hardest and demanded perfection from the underclassmen. At times, the competition was so fierce that fights often broke out between teammates during practice. I had never witnessed first-hand individuals give so much effort to accomplish a goal.

For four years, I dedicated my time to perfecting my basketball skills. It wasn't until my senior year that the hard work finally paid off. I was taller, stronger, faster, and more confident. When pre-season workouts began, I outworked my teammates placing first in almost every race. My skills had developed significantly as well. During a preseason game, I performed so well that for the first time my coach informed me that I had a shot to play college basketball if I continued working hard on and off the court.

Unfortunately, my performance off the court was less inspiring. In the classroom, I was a mediocre student at best. I completed my assignments and did just enough studying to pass tests, but I barely produced above and beyond C-level work. I held a 2.5 GPA for most of my high school career and I scored a nineteen on the ACT on the first try without studying. The two were more than enough to qualify me for a basketball scholarship and so I only cared to maintain that average. This mind-set was pervasive amongst many of my teammates who viewed academic achievement as a necessary evil to play basketball. Despite my lukewarm grades and test scores, I applied and gained admittance to several schools, but I was only interested in colleges where I had a chance to play basketball. In my social life, like most seniors, I had reached the pinnacle of high school popularity. With this newfound fame came the attraction of girls. I found myself in a relationship with a young lady who I met when I was working at a local grocery and we became inseparable throughout the school year. For the first time, basketball began to take a back seat as puppy love edged out my focus. Eventually, my lack of concentration led to poor performance on the court and I was benched for much of the year. The nadir came on senior night when the coach refused to put me in the game despite the obvious symbolic importance of the contest. Two games away from the end of the season, I quit the team.

Although I quit the team, I knew my basketball career was far from over. I learned that my high school's track coach was well connected in the basketball recruiting scene, so I joined the track team for the first time as a senior and ran the 800-meter relay with three other underclassman who also played basketball and were natural track stars. I applied the same work ethic I developed playing basketball to running track and soon became an asset to the team. Our 800-meter team prevailed in several meets; we even placed top five in the lauded Texas relays. When the season ended, the rumors about the track coach's connections proved accurate as he rewarded my hard-work by coordinating a basketball tryout for me with a small school in Tennessee.

My high school coach's pre-season assessment of my abilities proved true when I received a basketball scholarship to play for Bethel College in McKenzie, Tennessee. I was one of a handful of my teammates to get an opportunity to play college basketball and I worked feverishly over the summer in preparation for my freshman year. Three of my close friends from Memphis were also set to attend the same college and play basketball; we held each other accountable that summer by pushing each other to our limits with training and conditioning. When school started in the fall, I was ready to do battle on the court, but I soon realized how unprepared I was for the academic war that lied ahead. I didn't understand the importance of using a syllabus to track my progress throughout the semester. I struggled to keep up with the reading assignments which often consisted of hundreds of pages a night for several classes. I had not developed proper study habits for test preparation such as creating outlines for classes or joining study groups. These were all skills that I could tell many of my classmates had mastered before matriculating; I watched as they breezed through exams and earned high marks. School seemed as second nature to them as a layup was to me. Add the difficulty of three-a-day practices to my existing academic woes and it's a miracle I survived my first semester. To make things even more interesting, I came home to visit my family in November to find out that my ex-girlfriend in high school had given birth to a child. The child was mine and he was already three weeks old.

My second year in college I transferred to be closer to my newly discovered responsibilities. I had not given up on my hoop dreams yet; I decided to try-out for a local university in my hometown and managed to make the team. It was a step up in competition from my previous school, so making the team was a major accomplishment. However, the coach did not offer me a scholarship, so I relied on grants and student loans to finance my tuition. The school was also more academically rigorous than my previous college, and I continued to struggle in class. Many of my credits hadn't transferred to my new school and, as a result, I was virtually a freshman again. By spring semester, my grades were only fractionally above a 2.0 and I had received a 1.9 in the fall. When I returned home that summer, I knew I had reached a crossroads in my education. I realized that I would never graduate unless I quit basketball and put all my efforts into school. I rarely saw any playing time anyway and the coach had no intentions of making me a scholarship player. It was that spring semester of 2003 that I let my dream of playing college basketball die. I had accomplished more with the sport than I could have ever imagined given my late start, but it was time to move on.

Enlightenment

As my focus shifted from basketball to other endeavors, I found myself with more time on my hands. Unlike my previous college, my new school's student body was much more diverse. For the first time, I became friends with students whose primary focus was not sports. My close friends consisted of engineering, accounting, IT, business, and history majors with visions of careers beyond college. Like me, they enjoyed sports and hip-hop music, but they also conversed about politics, economics, and social issues that impacted the black community. They looked like me and we shared most of the same values, but they also excelled academically. At the end of my junior year, a few of my closest college friends started attending non-university affiliated group meetings led by a black radiologist and historian. The group met in a dilapidated building in the heart of South Memphis, one of the poorest neighborhoods in the city. The structure held about seventy-five people at capacity and usually exceeded that number during meetings. My friends and I looked forward to the tasty southern food that the venue provided. The smell of collard greens, baked chicken, yams, and black-eyed peas permeated the room as we ate and watched documentaries on African-American history and racism in the U.S. The films opened my eyes to the systemic racism that has existed in the U.S. since the days of forced labor. I learned about government initiatives such as COINTELPRO and read about the government's role in preventing minorities from establishing political power. Other meetings focused on religion and its impact on black people as a culture. One meeting focused on the etymology of words and the psychological impact that words have on its users. Many of the sessions focused on African history and how intelligent, creative, and powerful black people have continued to be since the beginning of time. Lawyers, doctors, scientists, teachers, college students, high school students, factory workers attended the meetings, and most of them were people of color. For the first time, I was inspired to learn for my own personal enjoyment and edification. I was beginning to make the connection between education and personal fulfillment. There was so much that I didn't know about the world and I started to realize that my imagination, and ultimately my aspirations, had been limited by my own ignorance. I began reading dozens of books on topics ranging from race to personal finance. I took school more seriously and implemented several study strategies I adopted from the group. My last four semesters in college I received a 3.0 or higher average; one semester I received a 3.5 and eventually graduated with a 2.5 GPA after pulling it up from a 1.9. I went on to attend graduate school and finished with a 3.9 GPA.

My success in college only made me more confident that I had been selling myself short academically. My potential lied dormant all those years waiting for inspiration to shake it from its slumber. Once I realized that I could apply the same dedication and discipline that I had applied to basketball to achieve any goal in life, I was no longer afraid of failure. More important, I came to understand that my race did not dictate my trajectory. Seeing successful professional people who looked and talked like me and who shared similar values changed my life. It was an experience I imagine other students encountered daily perhaps not even realizing its psychological impact. I thought back to the early 90s when I was an adolescent. One of my favorite television shows was *A Different World*, a sitcom depicting the daily lives of students on the campus of a fictional historically black college named Hillman. The characters all had different majors and passions ranging from pre-med to law. By the end of the final season, many of the characters had become working professionals. I didn't understand until much later the importance of watching black men and women depicted in a college setting in a non-exploitative way. Later in life, Howard University School of Law would become my real-life Hillman experience further cementing a positive identity as a black man.

In 2013, I graduated Howard Law School at the top of my class and went on to work at one of the top law firms in the country. On paper, I appeared to be a prime example of the opportunities available to everyone living in a meritocracy, but I knew that my experience was the exception and not the rule. By the time I finished law school, many of my high school classmates were dead or in jail. For those who had dodged the cemetery and the penitentiary, most dropped out of or never attended college and ended up confined to manual labor. I felt a sense of survivor's guilt the higher I climbed up the professional ladder. I knew my success was largely a result of fortune. I had been lucky to transfer schools and find a coach who valued hard work over skill. Sports kept me out of trouble and offered me a chance to attend college. Living in a single parent household with a father who, at the time, had no income was a blessing in disguise as low-income grants financed most of my education. I had been lucky to find a peer group who embraced me and showed me a different perspective on life. Many of my peers were not as fortunate. Despite the money I was making, I felt a nagging sense of duty to give back to my community.

The Spook Who Sat by the Door

During my second year at the firm, I received a phone call from a close friend about an opportunity to take a position as a federal prosecutor. Initially, I scoffed at the thought of taking a significant pay-cut to work in a broken system but after a few weeks I reconsidered.

One night, while lying half asleep in my bed, I reflected on the movie *The Spook Who Sat by the Door* —a political satire that I was exposed to during the Afrocentric meetings I attended during undergrad. The film was based on Sam Greenlee's 1968 novel with the same name. It depicted a story about a black man who was accepted into the CIA through a program designed to satisfy a recent quota require-ment of the agency. During his time in the CIA, he discovered many of the agency's secret tactics and, after quitting the force, used those skills to train African-American teens in Chicago on how to execute guerrilla warfare in American cities to bring about political change. The book and movie were banned in the US by the FBI during the civil rights movement of the late 60s and early 70s due to their subversive themes. I always wanted an opportunity to become my own version of the Spook in Greenlee's film—to learn as much as possible about the system and use that information to train others to avoid and destroy its trappings. I would infiltrate the system and help as many people as I could without being detected or brainwashed. I would administer justice my way; the way I believed the criminal justice system should work.

I decided to leave "Big Law" and enter the field of criminal law as a prosecutor. I knew that I owed it to my family, friends and everyone in my childhood community to use my law degree to create change. I longed for the spiritual fulfillment of helping others avoid the circumstances that befell many of my family members, friends, and classmates. For two and a half years, I became entangled in the web of the criminal justice system. I discovered realities that challenged my assumptions about the system. I struggled with the internal conflict of identifying as a black man while simultaneously sending black men to prison. Ironically, the competitive nature that I developed playing sports often impeded my ability to adminis-ter justice fairly. I describe the stories of victims and defendants whose life changing experiences also became my own. These are the memoirs of my life changing journey as a black prosecutor in the U.S.'s criminal justice system.

EMPATHY

*"We need someone who's got the heart, the empathy,
to recognize what it's like to be a young teenage mom,
the empathy to understand what it's like to be poor or
African-American or gay or disabled or old – and that's
the criterion by which I'll be selecting my judges."*

—BARACK OBAMA

As a prosecutor, you are the most powerful and thus must be the most open-minded agent in the criminal justice system. At the core of your responsibilities is to ferret out the truth and determine when people in our society have violated the laws established to protect the public, and more importantly how to approach any violations of those laws. Ultimately, your decision could determine whether a person is ever allowed to hold a valid driver's license, able to vote, and/or in some cases ever breathe again. These decisions are never as simple as applying the black letter law to a set of facts or analyzing a person's criminal history and placing him or her in a box within the sentencing guidelines. These decisions go to the core of who you are as a person; how you were raised, what you believe, and your personal experiences. If a prosecutor's duty is to protect and serve the community by preventing crime and punishing those who commit them, then it is imperative that he or she understand the people in those communities and what motivates their behavior in society. Empathy is what helps prosecutors answer the question of why this person deserves a second chance or why this person should not be spared the sword. Truthfully, it is much easier to forgive those whose actions we can relate to or justify in our own minds, but when we look at someone and think of them as different from us or inherently evil, we cannot fairly judge them.

I can recall overhearing two colleagues discussing a case in the hallway. One was a white female who had grown up comfortably, lived in middle-class neighborhoods her entire life, and attended nice schools. She was speaking about one of her defendant's being shot a few weeks after our office had charged him with an unrelated drug offense. In her mind, the guy was clearly a "bad guy" who was involved in nefarious activities. "People don't just get shot for no reason," she exclaimed. It was clear that she had never ventured outside of her comfort zone or lived in places where people get shot quite frequently for doing nothing at all or at least nothing that would warrant them catching a bullet—a fact that I knew very well narrowly avoiding gunfire myself and knowing friends who hadn't been so lucky. In her mind though, this was yet another example of her defendant's own life choices. He was caught selling drugs and so he must have been doing something wrong when he was shot, because, to her, drug dealing and violence obviously go hand-in-hand.

Although it is true that the judge levies the final sentence, much of the damage is already done by the time a person is found guilty. The prosecutor determines who will be charged, what the charges will be, and whether to continue pursuit of those charges. I have seen cases dropped for nothing more than the whims of a supervisor or the recommendations of a prosecutor who felt the need to show compassion for a defendant. I've also seen misdemeanor-worthy felony charges remain as felonies because our office labeled the defendant a "bad guy" or the case simply fell into the wrong prosecutor's hands. It wasn't so much that there was a pervasive culture of incarcerate-them-all—although I did come to know a few people who appeared to hold this view —it was more so a lack of a connection between the accused and the accuser. Many of my colleagues had never experienced the despair of not knowing where they were going to lay their heads down at night. All many of them had ever known were dual-parent households where the biggest dilemma was determining which college they would attend and what profession they would pursue. Few of them had experienced the psychological impact of neglect, physical abuse, or malnourishment. They saw only the action, the result of a man or woman who had made poor choices in life. Many of my colleagues were disillusioned by the falsehood that the U.S was a meritocracy that offered all its citizens free choices. This is not to say that there were no prosecutors that I worked with who held compassion for defendants. In fact, I believe many of my fellow prosecutors made genuine attempts to place themselves in the shoes of their defendants, but undoubtedly the task was made more difficult for those from starkly different cultural backgrounds.

The importance of empathy in the carrying out of a prosecutor's duties does not rest solely with how his or her actions will impact the defendant. To the contrary, the ability to understand and connect with victims may be equally, if not more, important. Without a victim to serve as a witness in court, your chances of winning a criminal case are slim to none. The strength of your case will largely rise and fall with how cooperative your victim and other witnesses are in your case. Many times, a prosecutor is asking her victims to share with a stranger an extremely vulnerable, embarrassing, and painful experience. Several of the violent crimes that I prosecuted involved a diverse makeup of victims including: a transgendered male, a drug addict, an undocumented U.S. resident, a prostitute, a homeless man, and a business owner. My experience has been that victims are not overly excited about working with law enforcement in the first place and would much rather move on with their lives. In fact, in some communities it was taboo to cooperate with law enforcement in anyway and breaking that code resulted in deadly consequences. Consequently, it was imperative for me to build trust with my victims quickly to gain their compliance without using the threat of a subpoena. If I had come across as judgmental, apathetic or overly concerned with my own self-interest, there was no way I would get them to tell the truth about their case or cooperate with me. My first few months as a prosecutor, I often rushed right into the case while speaking with victims and foolishly expected their cooperation. But as I gained more experience, I changed my approach. I rarely started the conversation discussing the case. I would ask about their day and engage in small talk to let them know that I cared about them on a personal level. This tactic didn't work for everyone, but I noticed more success gaining cooperation. I also realized that many of my victims were African Americans who shared my life experiences. I noticed a certain level of comfort when they saw my face and realized that we spoke the same "language". It was my ability to understand their situation that helped me gain trust and compliance from many of them.

Empathy not only plays an important role in building rapport with victims, but it also determines whether prosecutors zealously pursue cases. For a year, I worked in the domestic violence ("DV") unit. In my opinion, DV is the most taxing unit in any DA's office. In the majority of the DV cases I prosecuted, the victims were completely uncooperative. Many of them failed to appear in court or if they did, they had no problem committing perjury to exonerate their lover or family member. DV prosecutors often found themselves in a seemingly unwinnable battle with the defense attorney and their own victim. Without an understanding of the cycle of violence and the dependency that many of these victims had experienced, it would have been easy for a prosecutor to give up on them and drop these cases. This issue arose in other types of cases as well.

I remember one case where a group of black men were listening to loud music outside of a recently gentrified neighborhood. Instead of calling the police, the newly minted resident went downstairs to confront the group. Apparently, the intoxicated man spouted a few choice racial slurs towards the group that were not well received. The men commenced to assaulting the man in front of his wife.

The injuries were severe enough to warrant felony charges, but I was inclined to drop them. In my mind, the victim deserved every blow. When I met with the victim, he never admitted to uttering the racial slurs, but I could tell by his body language that he was lying. Despite my acrimony for his actions, I couldn't ignore the permanent scars to his face and head nor could I overlook how emotional scarred his wife was from the experience. I decided that misdemeanors were more appropriate charges to file and I got the young men's cases dropped to misdemeanors with no jail time.

This is the delicate balance that is required of a prosecutor daily. Without the ability to step into the shoes of victims and defendants alike, there is no way you can carry out your duty of administering justice effectively.

1

IN ANOTHER LIFE, WE WOULD HAVE BEEN BEST FRIENDS

I was sitting alone at the wooden table designated for the prosecution, with the jury to my left and the defense table to my right. The feeling of angst that I usually experienced while awaiting a verdict was oddly absent. I sat there staring straight ahead blankly in a mostly vacant courtroom but for five other people: the judge, the defendant, his attorney, a U.S. Marshall and the courtroom clerk. In hindsight, my perceived stoicism was more a feeling of relief that the trial was finally over than anything else. My caseload consisted of over thirty felony cases and I had worked countless hours to retry this case. I thought to myself, this one at least would not end in a hung jury as it had before, whether innocent or guilty I now had one less case on my docket. After about a minute of sitting in complete silence, the faint sound of knocking emerged from inside the jury deliberation room signaling that the jurors were ready to read the verdict. The parties stood as the jury entered the room. My custom before a verdict was to try to get a sense for their decision by looking into the juror's eyes when they entered the room; if they avoided eye contact with the defendant, I felt there was a high likelihood I had prevailed. If the jurors avoided eye contact with me, I figured the chance of a conviction was slim. Despite the obvious flaws to this litmus test; I scanned each juror's face in hopes of an indication of the verdict. None of the jurors gave me eye contact—surely a sign of defeat. But it didn't take long for me to second guess my initial premonition.

It is customary in jury trials for a foreperson to emerge as the leader during deliberations. This person is typically someone the other jurors look up to or respect because he or she possesses leadership qualities and/or some specific knowledge about the issues of the case, e.g. he or she is a criminal lawyer in a murder trial or a doctor in a medical malpractice case. Truth be told, it is difficult to predict who the jurors will select as their foreperson, but generally that person's view of the case will impact everyone else's.

My foreperson emerged from juror seat number six. He was a bald, rotund middle-aged white man. I put a smiley face beside his name in my notes during jury selection. Throughout his twenty-year career, he worked closely with law enforcement and, unlike many other government friendly jurors, number six possessed enough savvy to answer the judge's questions during voir dire (jury selection questioning) so as not to reveal an obvious bias in favor of law enforcement. This prevented the defense from challenging the juror "for cause", a challenge the defense-friendly judge would have swiftly granted with even a hint of bias. Nonetheless, I was sure that my opponent would use one of his strikes to eliminate number six.

The defendant's attorney, Mr. Colt, was a seasoned trial lawyer with decades of experience as a prosecutor and even more years as a criminal defense attorney. His crafty advocacy produced a 10-2 hung jury in the first trial and he was confident he would secure an acquittal, but even Mr. Colt's usual confident demeanor waned when he observed juror number six rise. The crux of my case depended upon the jury's acceptance of my police officers' testimony. Colt had all but allowed a law enforcement official on his jury; a misstep that was written all over his face when juror number six emerged as the foreperson.

Juror number six walked over and handed the verdict sheet to the judge's clerk who then handed the verdict to the judge and then in reverse back to juror number six. I continued to stare off into the distance not wanting to make eye contact with the judge to avoid the awkwardness and not wanting to stare at the jury or the defense for the same reason. As the judge asked the jury their verdict on each count, the word guilty followed each request. At that moment, I felt validation. All my hard-work and preparation had manifested into tangible results. The judge who had derided me throughout both trials failed miserably at disguising her contempt for the verdict. For ten entire seconds, I felt happy. I hadn't taken the time to look at the defense attorney or his client, but when I finally did my glee quickly faded. The defendant stood with his head down visibly furious with the outcome; he stared at the ground with a sense of defeat and anger that I could only imagine. I started to think about his case and wondered, what if he was telling the truth? What if somehow, I had convicted an innocent man? I knew I was being a bit dramatic. I had enough evidence to convince twelve people of his guilt and deep down inside I felt that he was guilty, but when I looked into his eyes I couldn't help but think about a familiar face.

Riding Dirty in Memphis

It was the summer of 2004 and my best friend Tony recalls riding with his brother (Joe) and cousin (Derrick) in his 1986 Nissan Maxima on a hot summer night. Tony promised to take Joe and Derrick out for Derrick's 18th birthday. Derrick was finally old enough to enter the strip club and since neither Joe nor Derrick had transportation, Tony became the prime candidate to serve as their chaperone.

Diamonds was not your typical strip club. Undercover police had shut down the establishment on multiple occasions for prostitution.

Somehow, the new owners repeatedly reopened the club, changed the name but kept the same business model. The voluptuous dancers spent as much time soliciting on the floor as they did stripping on the stage and there was no shortage of demand. Even as "shake junt" newbies, the three were aware of what took place in those dark rooms where a revolving door of men and women existed.

Before Tony left the house to pick up his brother Joe, he laced up his Nikes and threw on some baggy pants and a Roca-wear T-shirt. He reached under his pillow and grabbed his loaded .40 caliber Ruger and tucked it into his waistband before walking to his car and placing it in the console. Memphis was a dangerous city and the fear of death outweighed the fear of a felony. The city was known for senseless killings. From the late 90s to the early 2000s, Memphis had a Wild-West feel to it. It seemed that everyone owned or at least possessed a gun and had no qualms about using it. Not to mention, trouble had its way of finding Tony whenever he decided to go out with his brother and cousin. Tony had seen and heard enough shootings in his life to know that by the time the police arrived, it was too late. After placing the gun in the console, Tony headed to east Memphis to pick up Derrick and Joe.

When Tony arrived in east Memphis, Derrick and Joe were both excited. His brother emerged from the front door wearing a 2XL black T-shirt with blue jeans and a pair of Timberland boots. His cousin wore a red Ecko Unlimited T-shirt with Girbaud jeans and Air Force 1s.

The two jumped in the car and greeted Tony with warmth.

"What's the business fool?" Tony said.

"Mayne shit, let's hit the corner store on Perkins and get some drank," Joe replied.

"Yall niggas don't go too hard mayne, I ain't trying to get flapped."

Only Memphians would find this conversation comprehensible. The three of them clasped palms and embraced before buckling up for what they expected to be a wild night, one that Tony feared would take a turn for the worst. Tony dreaded having the gun in the car but the idea of needing it and not having it trumped those fears. His trepidations slowly began to materialize when his car pulled into the corner store. As the sole adult of drinking age in the car, Tony had the esteemed duty of purchasing liquor for the group—not that their ages really mattered; Tony was purchasing liquor at the age of seventeen from a store nearby for years without as much as a glance at his face from the clerk. The owner knew Tony and his friends by name and never once asked for ID.

Derrick and Joe were already drinking a small bottle of gin during the ride to the gas station, so Tony pulled over to the 711 to buy something to last them the rest of the night. He opened his door and told his brother and cousin to stay in the car. When he got into the store, he spotted the "two elevens" in the rear refrigerator and grabbed a twelve pack. Two elevens were notorious for their high alcohol content and low price, a perfect combination for a struggling college student on a $15 budget.

When he returned to the parking lot, Tony witnessed the gin taking effect. Joe had turned up the music so loud that the car windows were shaking. Tony could see his brother and cousin inside rocking back and forth to the music. He put the two elevens in the car and turned down the music a notch before starting to fill up his tank. Before he could finish pumping gas, Derrick had flung open the car door. He hopped out of the car after apparently taking issue with the look he received from a random white guy pumping his gas. Tony's cousin stepped up to the guy and swung like he was trying to hit a piñata, luckily, he missed. The poor guy looked horrified as he stared at what, to him, must have been three black guys with every intention of taking his life if he retaliated.

"Fuck you. Muh da fucking white boy!" exclaimed Tony's cousin.

"Man, why the hell you do that?" Tony lamented.

"Jones ass should not have been looking crazy bruh. I shoulda smacked his ass." responded Derrick.

The entire time, Joe surveyed the situation intently from his passenger seat waiting for his cue to enter the fray. Eventually the poor middle-aged man angrily fled the scene in his Honda Accord and avoided the three of them having to make his night even worse. In that instant, Tony reflected on all of the white people he encountered on the streets that walked to the other side when they saw him coming or who clinched their purses when they shared an elevator. It always angered him, but maybe people like his cousin were partly to blame. He had all but blackened this innocent man's eye whose only crime was looking in his direction. Tony was ashamed for a second, but only a second. Ten dollars filled the tank, so Tony twisted the gas top, closed the gas door, and returned the pump to its slot. The music from the car was blaring again as he entered the driver's seat and immediately realized that his brother had found his little secret within the console.

"Damn bruh, you got that fawty for a nigga ass don't you. Lemme see that junt," he exclaimed.

"Put that shit down bruh. I ain't trying to get flapped," Tony said.

"Nigga better not fuck with us tonight," Derrick chimed in the back seat with an open two eleven in his hand.

The gun was legally registered in Tony's name, but he had no license to carry it. Tony knew that the combination of a loaded weapon alongside driving with two under-aged drinkers in his car was a recipe for disaster, but he had promised his cousin and brother a good time and following through with his word meant everything to him. If this meant driving in a car while carrying a loaded weapon with underage drinkers, then so be it.

The drive was filled with unison chants of Yo Gotti lyrics over blaring bass and rattling speakers. Tony tried his best to reduce their chances of being pulled over by constantly reminding his intoxicated passengers to keep their bottles below window level while drinking. This rule was a lot easier to enforce while the two were sober—before they decided to mix gin and malt liquor. Now, keeping them in check was almost impossible. Tony's only chance was to take as many back streets as he possibly could to avoid police. He sped through yellow lights and pushed pass stop signs in neighborhoods to reach their destination as quickly as possible, making quick work of the trip.

Within fifteen minutes, Tony arrived about two blocks away from Lamar Avenue where two of Memphis' most popular businesses were located: UPS and Diamonds. Tony was racing over rocky railroad tracks while his teenage comrades were insanely intoxicated in the back seat. The bumps in the road had turned their joyfully faces into an ominous green hue. A disturbing silence resonated in the car and it only took Tony a few minutes to realize what was about to happen.

"Man, yall better not throw up in my car. I told yall fools not to drink all those beers"

"We good bruh. We good dog," said Joe in a pathetically weak tone.

"We there yet Tony mayne? I need to pee like a motherfucker," Derrick whimpered.

Luckily, they had finally arrived at the club. Tony took a soft right into the no-named dead-end street where the club was located. He slowly pulled near the club. Judging by the parking lot it was already jam packed. Parked near the street was a Crown Victoria with twenty-two-inch rims and chameleon paint. The windows were so darkly tinted that Tony could see his own reflection in them. There was an all-black Cadillac truck parked with two wheels propped up on the curb to the left of the parking lot. Tony decided to park his car in a place that offered an easy exit in case the three needed to make a quick escape. He could recall the time the three of them were walking on Beale Street and a shooting incited a stampede that almost cost them their lives; it was simply one of dozens of shootings outside of clubs that they had narrowly escaped. Tony backed into a slot on the curbside behind the Cadillac with the hood of his car facing Democrat Road. He would be the first car out granted they made it to the car. Joe stumbled out of the car and decided to take a piss in the nearby shrubbery and Derrick soon followed suit. Tony thought about joining them, but cars were driving by and he was not yet drunk enough to expose himself to the public no matter how much pressure his bladder was experiencing. Tony encouraged them to speed up.

"Man, yall niggas could have waited five minutes to get in the club," Tony said "Hell naw bruh. Ahhhhhhhh!" Joe expressed while releasing a liter of 211. "Let's go get on these strippers cuz," said Derrick.

They headed towards the entrance. There stood a brown complexioned security guard with a pit-bullish demeanor carrying a nine-millimeter handgun on his waist. His size made the gun look like a miniature version of itself. They watched as he frisked patrons from head to toe, groping pockets and waving his metal-detecting wand over their bodies. They reached the front as the 6'5 three-hundred-pound monstrosity gave them an incredulous look. Tony prayed security would deny them entry and end his chaperon duties for the night. He could tell that the guard either questioned their ages or noticed how inebriated his underage comrades appeared. Tony hoped the guard would ask them to leave, but sadly the guard looked down at each of their licenses, looked back up at their faces and proceeded to frisk them. After the search, the bouncer nodded toward the ticket desk inside where they paid a combined $50 to enter the club. Entry for patrons too young to drink was an extra $10 since the club could not legally sell them drinks, even though they could illegally purchase sex. Of age patrons were only charged $10, because they were required to purchase a minimum of two drinks to remain in the club which made being underage the better bargain.

After dropping the entry fee with the half-dressed door lady, the triad entered an oasis of debauchery. Southern Rap was blasting through enormous subwoofers. Women were either completely naked or only wearing a top with no bottom or vice versa but no one had on a full uniform. Men of all ages were inside. Many of them were hovered around the dance floor with a drink in one hand and a fist full of cash in the other. Some enjoyed watching in awe as the women effortlessly climbed the polls and levitated themselves while showcasing their perfectly shaped bodies. Other patrons preferred to touch and used money as bait to get the women to sit in their laps while they gently placed mint green paper in their G-strings.

It didn't take long for security to realize Joe and Derricks' level of intoxication once they got inside. Neither one of them had any money (and neither did Tony) but that didn't stop either one of them from touching the women or picking up money off the ground and using it as their own. Once the club staff picked up on it, they approached Tony and told him that he needed to get them out of the club. The request made Tony upset because he had finally gotten one of the strippers to sit in his lap despite his lack of funds. Still, this wasn't the worst news he had heard all night. He finally had an excuse to leave before things got out of hand. He was in the back of the club when he noticed his brother bending over a trash can near the front. His cousin was in a similar position, but he was kneeled over a chair near the front stage. Within seconds, Tony knew what was happening: the two were throwing up their insides in front of everyone. The girls were screaming and running towards the back where Tony stood as male staff watched visibly upset. Security recognized Tony as the soberest out the group. After a few minutes of puking, the two were clearly nauseous and staggering. Club staff had brought out two mops by the time Tony had finally gotten the two on their feet, so they could leave when …

"Ah naw cuz, you finna clean this shit up," said the manager.

"That's not my job," Tony said.

"Nigga, you brought them in here," the manager retorted.

Tony looked around and realized that both bouncers were standing nearby, one next to the manager, the other behind him. They hadn't said a word, but Tony knew what their presence meant: either he clean up or the bouncers would kick them out and the kicking would not be figurative. Tony decided to swallow his pride and proceeded to clean up the vomit while most of the club watched.

The music was still loud, but the lights were on so that Tony could see the spots that needed cleaning. This of course had the effect of making him the center of attention in the club. The dancers and patrons stared as he mopped up the pool of mush. The smell of the disinfectant and vomit made Tony want to hurl, but he finished up as quickly as possible, grabbed his disoriented brother and cousin and stormed out of the club as everyone watched and laughed. As Tony passed the pit-bull faced bouncer on the way out, the guard cracked a condescending smile and shook his head at the group.

When they got back to the car, Tony was fuming with anger. He had been "punked" in front of the entire club and forced to clean every inch of puke off the floors. His brother was half conscious in the passenger seat while his cousin was raving in the back of the car incoherently.

"Tony man, bust the fawty at them niggas bruh!" said Derrick as he grabbed for the console.

Tony pushed him back and pressed his elbow against the console tightly so that his cousin couldn't open it. He watched the bouncer from about fifty feet away still laughing in their direction. It took everything in him not to take his cousin's suggestion. He wanted more than anything to wipe that smile off the security guard's face and make the bouncers feel the fear that he felt when he was surrounded in the club. Instead, Tony told his cousin to sit back and put his seatbelt on.

That night Tony took his brother and cousin home around 5:00 a.m. and made it into his apartment at 5:30 a.m. He was lucky the police hadn't pulled him over that night. He could count several reasons why they would have been justified to search his car and would have found his gun in the console. He would have had no choice but to plea to a felony and endure all of the collateral consequences that flow from it. The consequences that awaited my defendant.

Still in a daze thinking about the irony of prosecuting this defendant, I hadn't heard the judge's question. When I looked over at the defendant, all I could see was Tony's face staring back at me.

"Mr. Jackson, what is your position on release pending sentencing?" said the judge.

No Easy Decision

For these types of cases, our office routinely sought incarceration pending sentencing, particularly in felony gun cases for repeat offenders. Although Marcus—my recently convicted defendant—had no previous gun convictions, police observed him on several occasions with what appeared to be a gun in his possession. However, Marcus beat the charges by fleeing police and tossing the gun away before his eventual arrest. Juries regularly acquitted in these "dropsee" cases, especially without DNA or fingerprint evidence to tie the defendant to the gun. After rolling the dice in three trials, Marcus' luck had finally run out.

In my case, Marcus found himself riding in the back seat of a Cadillac at 2:00 a.m. with three women he recently met on Instagram. Apparently, the police observed the female driver passing by without a seatbelt and pulled the car over for a traffic violation. When the car came to a stop, Marcus jumped out and immediately took off running. Officer Taylor pursued him down the courtyard of the nearby apartments. Midway through the chase, Marcus pitched a gun into the bushes and, seconds later, officers waiting on the other side of the courtyard, arrested him. Once again, no DNA or fingerprint evidence existed, but this time we had an officer observe the gun in Marcus' hand and recovered the gun right near the bushes.

At the first trial, I pondered the defense's strategy. Mr. Colt would have to argue that the police were lying but I couldn't figure out how. Marcus would need to explain the coincidence of police finding a gun in the nearby bushes seconds after his arrest. When Mr. Colt presented his first witness, their strategy became more apparent. He started by calling one of Marcus' best friends, Jermichael, who testified about numerous incidents where Officer Taylor had allegedly assaulted Marcus. Jermichael was around eighteen years old, slender with a box fade. He wore black and white Jordan retro 12s with skinny jeans and a baggy white T-shirt. Jermichael described with detail one incident where Officer Taylor allegedly pulled Marcus down by his locks and slammed him to the ground. Jermichael testified with conviction that after this initial incident, "Officer Jordan" (a name people in the neighborhood had given Officer Taylor for his resemblance to the former NBA player) had it out for Marcus. After Jermichael left the stand, the defense called a second witness, Phillip, another best friend of the defendant. Phillip was a tall, dark-skinned young man with a low haircut. He was older than Jermichael and more confident on the stand. Phillip gave the same account as Jermichael, save a few inconsistencies that I attempted to exploit but weren't overly damaging to their case.

The police corruption defense was becoming more popular, especially with the spike in police shootings around the country of unarmed black men. Marcus' defense that Officer Taylor had it out for him and planted the gun in the bushes to see Marcus go to jail proved effective, as I watched the jury's nodding heads of approval. The icing on the cake came when Marcus took the stand. His locks were pulled back in a ponytail and he wore a polo short-sleeve shirt tucked into khaki pants. He had a sense of humor and came across as a charming young man. He had the jury eating out of his hand by the time I started my cross. The jury took two days before they hung, 10-2 in favor of conviction. I had gotten close but not close enough.

Marcus and his attorney were confident that if the jury hung a second time, we would drop the case. They were probably right, but unfortunately for Marcus, I had done my homework this time. Giving a prosecutor a second bite at the apple, is a defense attorney's worst nightmare. I now possessed sworn testimony to pick apart months in advance of trial. I exploited inconsistencies in their testimony. I even read through an old drug case file where Marcus was convicted for possession of marijuana. In this misdemeanor case, Marcus ran from police and got caught with a small amount of weed on his person. During the pursuit, the officers (one black) were forced to tackle him to the ground causing Marcus to bite a hole in his tongue from the force of the fall. I knew I needed to bait Marcus into lying on the stand to destroy the choir boy act that he had put on for the jury in the previous trial, but I couldn't find a lie that I could disprove. Suddenly, during the re-trial, he began describing one of the alleged assaults by Officer Taylor, I questioned him about the injuries he received from the assaults.

"So, what type of injuries did you receive when Officer Jordan, as you call him, assaulted you?" I asked.

"He pulled one of my dreads out. I actually still have a hole in my tongue from when he slammed my face into the ground," he said sheepishly.

I paused for a minute and smiled. The entire courtroom watched me with puzzled looks on their faces as I walked over to my table and grabbed a photo from the desk. I strolled over to the defense table to show Mr. Colt the photo and immediately drew an objection. We approached the bench and spoke with the judge.

"Your honor, the defense objects to the use of this photo on relevance grounds. What is the relevance of this photo of my client?" said defense counsel.

"Your honor, this witness has testified about the injuries that he received from an alleged assault by one of the witnesses in the government's case. This photo is from an unrelated arrest and it will establish that the defendant did not receive the hole in his tongue from Officer Taylor, but rather from running from police, on a separate occasion. This is impeachment evidence your honor." I said.

"Your honor! There is no way that the government can establish that this is my client in this photo or that any of these things happened. I object based on a lack of foundation your honor," Mr. Colt exclaimed.

"Your honor, we have the officers here who arrested the defendant on the day he injured his tongue. They recognize the defendant and remember the arrest. They also remember taking the photo. Furthermore, the defendant may establish that this is him in the photo," I retorted.

"Mr. Colt, I don't see a basis for excluding this evidence. Your objection is "overruled".

You may proceed, Mr. Jackson," stated the judge.

When I approached Marcus with the photo in hand, he looked over to Mr. Colt and could tell that something was wrong. Mr. Colt had his right hand pressed against his forehead staring blankly into the defense table and made no eye contact with the court. Marcus continued to stare at Mr. Colt while I asked him the question, until eventually he refocused his attention on the photo.

"Marcus, this is you in this photo isn't it?" I said.

"Yes," he said, perplexed.

"And this photo is showing a hole in your tongue, correct?" I stated.

"Yes," he said.

"And this hole in your tongue didn't come from Officer Taylor, did it?" I said.

"No," he said.

I took the photo from the table and rested. Once I presented the testimony of the black officer who arrested Marcus to establish— 1) Marcus did not receive the hole in his tongue from Officer Taylor, and 2) (and perhaps more importantly) Marcus had run-ins with black officers as well— the case was won. Mr. Colt had no follow up questions for his client. He knew it was all over. The jury's posture changed. They no longer made eye contact with the defendant. Marcus' lie destroyed his credibility.

"Mr. Jackson, what is your position on the defendant's release pending sentencing?" the judge repeated as I snapped out of my trance.

"Your honor, let's give him an opportunity to show the court that he deserves probation in this case. The government has no objection to release," I said hesitantly.

"Very well. Mr. Mitchell, the court is going to release you because the government isn't asking that you remain in prison. You are on a very short leash here. If you so much as breathe too hard, I will have no choice but to lock you up until your next court date," said the judge.

I walked out of the courtroom feeling conflicted. I had won a difficult case, but I had also contributed to the broken system. A felony for Marcus would mean relegation to a social caste system preventing him from any meaningful opportunities at living a productive life. My experience growing up around friends who carried guns illegally for protection allowed me to empathize with Marcus' life choices. He grew up in a place where he witnessed his cousin murdered right in front of him. Like Tony and myself, Marcus grew up in a neighborhood where innocent people were victimized as frequently as those deserving of retaliation. Often, a gun served as the only hope of avoiding an untimely death.

I released Marcus because I saw my best friend, and myself, in him. As I walked out of the doors of the courthouse and headed back to my office, I reflected on Tony's strip club experience and how things might have been different had the police pulled him over that night as they had done Marcus. For Tony, as is the case with many young adults, with age came wisdom. He went on to finish college and became a successful real estate agent. He now lives in Memphis with his wife and kids. He coaches little league football in his free time and encourages kids to attend college. Marcus would not be so lucky, two months after his conviction, I discovered that he had picked up another gun charge while on release and committed an assault with a dangerous weapon against another inmate in prison. He would likely spend the better part of his twenties incarcerated.

2

HISTORY REPEATS ITSELF

My first caseload consisted of over one hundred domestic violence cases. All of which were in various stages of prosecution: many of the defendants were on probation or some type of diversion. Some were awaiting a plea agreement or sentencing. The others were pending a status hearing or trial. After a few months, I started to group the cases into three major categories: fighting, sexual, and property. Although the level of severity of each case varied greatly, the specific facts of each case rarely fell outside of one of these buckets; although at times the categories overlapped. Fighting comprised the largest of the three. I received fighting cases ranging from instances where the defendant spat on the victim to cases where the defendant beat the victim so badly that she needed structural surgery to her face. Sexual cases varied the most in severity; these cases could range from alleged groping on the metro to a sexual assault charged as a misdemeanor due to a lack of evidence or other flaws in the case. Property crimes were common as well and sometimes charged in tandem with other fighting type charges.

In the beginning, new cases presented unique and exciting facts for investigation. My mind became occupied with the tragedies of my victims. As a baby prosecutor, I often found myself waking up to dreams (sometimes nightmares) about cases that I handled. My social life consisted of happy hour conversations about the latest simple assault. But then, after a few months, the honeymoon ended. I became less interested in a black eye or a broken nose. Although my empathy for my victims remained (for the most part), I became numb to many of the facts of the cases and placed a higher premium on those cases with more serious injuries and more nefarious offenders. I felt a subtle competition amongst my peers to handle the most interesting cases, which typically meant the more serious injuries or more vulnerable victims. After a while, I began to view cases in terms of their value; each case came to me with a price tag ranging from a cheap simple assault to a valuable sexual assault. Despite this fact, I often came across "low value" cases that struck a nerve with me. These cases weren't going to earn me any stripes as a prosecutor because they were not high profile enough to garner any attention from supervisors but on a personal level they reminded me of my connectedness to the victims and defendants who came across my desk.

Michelle was one of those victims. I remember picking up her case and going through the regular routine of reading the affidavit and reviewing the defendant's criminal record to determine what type of plea offer I wanted to extend. The defendant's criminal history was non-existent, and there was no evidence, just the police paperwork. On paper, it appeared the defendant went into a jealous rage and choked the victim while she was in the bedroom. This prompted the victim to spray the defendant with pepper spray to get him out of the house. Apparently, at one point during the altercation, the defendant brandished a hammer in response to the pepper spray.

Sadly, I had seen worse. There was no indication that the defendant struck the victim with the hammer, so I was prepared to negotiate with the defense attorney to get rid of the case as quickly as possible. First, due to a federal statute, I needed to contact the victim and seek her input on what should happen in the case. I knew there was a fifty percent chance she either wouldn't answer the phone or would hang up on me once I identified myself, making my job that much easier. The phone rang and as expected it went to voicemail. I left the standard message explaining my role and that I would move forward with the case if I didn't hear from her within a week.

A week later, I received a call from a woman whose voice trembled with fear and anger all at once. When I announced my name, she began with an outburst:

"I don't want anything to do with no prosecution. Please drop this case, because I am not going forward. He is my boyfriend and I don't want him to go to jail," she said.

"Ma'am, I understand how you feel. What is your name again?" I replied.

"Michelle, you left a message on my phone last week. Look, just please drop this case, I'm not interested in going forward," she stated.

"Ma'm," I said as I tried to slip in a statement, but instead heard the dial tone.

I had grown accustomed to this colloquy, in fact, she was much more pleasant than most victims and now that I had fulfilled my statutory duty to attempt to inform her of her rights, I was free to dispose of the case. I figured I would take my time since the hearing was three weeks away. I put the case to the side and moved on to the next case. Another week passed when I received a phone call.

"Mr. Jackson? This is Michelle. I'm tired of James putting his hands on me. I want to move forward with the case. I don't want him to think he can keep doing this to me. He just keeps doing it. Plus, I want to get my daughter away from him. She shouldn't be around this. I'm tired, Mr. Jackson," the deflated voice said.

This was the first time that I became aware of a child's involvement. Michelle sounded unstable, which increased the likelihood of her experiencing a change of heart, especially if the defendant reconnected with her. I frequently witnessed victims return to the cycle of violence enticed by broken promises of change. I needed to get her out of her home and into safe housing.

"Ms. Davis, I'll connect you with one of our advocates. She will help you while I continue to investigate the case," I said.

By the time I hung up the phone, I had gotten the sense that the defendant's scant criminal record belied a history of assaults against Michelle. I made an expedited request for the photos and the 911 call in the case. A day later when they arrived, I immediately realized the seriousness of the case. As I began listening to the 911 call, waiting to hear Michelle's voice, I instead heard the terrified voice of Michelle's 9-year-old daughter pleading to the dispatcher for help and describing her mother's attack as it happened.

"He has a hammer! He's hurting my mom! Please come! Please! He's pressing the hammer against my mom's face," she cried.

This was the first I became aware that Michelle's daughter, Tiana, was watching the entire assault unfold. This case had suddenly become a high value case: an opportunity to work with a child victim and possibly put a child witness on the stand. Yet of course that was not at the forefront of my mind. That night, thoughts of Tiana's terrified voice over the phone besieged my conscious. I began to think back to my own childhood memories of domestic violence and how they shaped my formative and teenage years.

Life Father, Like Son

I was eight years old and it was one of the earliest memories I have of my mother and father dating. I vaguely recall a handful of restaurants to which my parents occasionally took me and my younger brother. Many of the meetings resulted in arguments between the two about things to which I paid little attention, but there were also times where they joked and showed each other compassion. My mom sometimes enjoyed my father's dark sense of humor, and she possessed enough charisma to stroke my father's ego.

However, I do remember one occasion that shaped my view of their relationship forever. We were riding in my father's pick-up truck near the riverfront. During the summer months, the area was a haven for couples in search of a romantic view of the Mississippi River flowing under the Hernando De Soto Bridge and moonlit sky. My brother, two years younger than me, was sound asleep in the back seat. He was notorious for his coma-like naps that required nothing short of yelling to bring him back to life. While he laid curled in the backseat, I sat wide awake perched forward from the back seat leaning half way into the front seat where the arm rest was positioned. Our car was parked on a grassy hill secluded from the main road but elevated enough to see the river.

Before long, it became clear to me that my mother and father were at odds. Tempers flared, and before I knew it, I found myself in the middle of their violent rage. I could see a level of anger in both of their eyes that I had never seen before, both yelling profanities at the top of their lungs. At some point, my mother had heard enough. She pulled a knife from her side and brandished it towards my father. I sat in the middle of them pleading for them both to stop, screaming at them both as my brother laid fast asleep. Soon I was crying hysterically fearing the worst would happen. Luckily, the altercation subsided, and no one was physically injured. Yet, the experience did leave a scar. I could notice my father's eyes swelled with tears not necessarily due to fear but assuredly because of the shame of watching his oldest son separate his parents from seriously injuring each other. It was at that point that I knew my parents would not be together and from that day forward, I never saw them together again.

Eleven years later history would repeat itself. I was a sophomore in college back at home living with family: my grandmother, father, uncle, and auntie all under one roof. The summer was one of the hottest I had experienced in my nineteen years as a Memphian and I could remember staying inside most of the day watching reruns of *A Different World* to avoid the heat wave. My father and I shared a room, but he was away, so I was lying in my bed when I heard the faint sound of my grandmother calling my name. I went to the door and as I got closer I could sense that something was wrong. My grandmother was staring outside of the screen door with both her hands placed firmly on her hips and hadn't noticed my presence, so she screamed my name again. I made myself known and brushed past her and noticed Jessica was standing in my driveway. I couldn't understand why my ex-girlfriend's cousin was at my house until I looked over her shoulder to observe my ex, Regina, with half her body outside of the driver side of her car yelling towards all three of us.

"Hey granny! You know Marty got me pregnant right?!" Regina exclaimed. "That's right, you trying to break up with me huh? Well, since you and Jessica such good friends, why don't you take her home!"

Jessica looked mortified listening to the exchange as she walked closer to the carport trying to explain her cousin's vocal onslaught the best way she could.

"Marty, you know she's crazy. I don't know why she brought me over here. I promise I told her to take me home," said Jessica.

I was paralyzed with feelings of anger and dismay. My grandmother stood there silent and undoubtedly equally perplexed. Shortly after the exchange, we watched Regina speed off leaving Jessica stranded in my driveway. I turned to my grandmother and used Jessica's presence to avoid the obvious questions that awaited.

"Granny, let me take Jessica home. I don't know what's wrong with that girl," I said.

We both hopped into the car and headed to Jessica's house.

I first met Jessica when I took Regina to her senior prom in 2002. Jessica needed a date and so I suggested that one of my friends, Donte, join us for a double prom date night. A year earlier, Regina and I first started dating during Regina's junior year and my senior of high school. We met through a mutual friend and things took off from there. I soon came to realize Regina's status as an only child who appeared to suffer from low self-esteem. I concluded that Regina's issues stemmed largely from her upbringing. Her mother drank frequently and, to make matters worse, a close relative allegedly molested Regina at a young age. I didn't know at the time, but I was her first boyfriend. Her mother was her only close family aside from her cousin. Despite her upbringing, Regina was a loving person. I admired her work ethic and generosity. At age 17, she worked 30+ hours a week at a restaurant to help her mom pay the bills while maintaining relatively good grades in school. She rarely made excuses and never had her hand out asking anyone for anything. Unfortunately, work ethic and benevolence weren't enough for a selfish teenage boy headed off to play college basketball. Being the mercurial teenager that I was, I decided to break things off the night of prom. I simply wouldn't have time for a girlfriend while away playing ball in college and I didn't want the relationship to linger the rest of the summer. Regina, visibly upset, cried for hours in the hotel. The tears fell on deaf ears. A few months later, I would leave for college with little to no remorse about breaking her heart.

A year later, we reunited after I returned home from college to my own family. Despite my past behavior and current predicament, Regina embraced me and ignored my troubles. She helped me find a job at a local thrift store. She picked me up and took me to work when my car needed repair. Unfortunately for Regina, it didn't take long before the college bug started to bite me again. Before long, I got back on my feet. That year I planned to matriculate to a local university closer to home where I might meet new people. I told Regina that the relationship was starting to suffocate me, but, in reality, it was July and I realized I was about to start school again. A new school with new friends and of course new women were all that was on my mind. Again, I broke it to her and told her that we needed a break; this time I did it over the phone. After about five minutes of enduring her yelling and screaming, I politely hung up my phone and turned it off for the night. I figured she would get over it after a while. I guess I was wrong.

"Can you take me to my friend's house first? I need to grab something," said Jessica.

Jessica's friend lived around the corner from my house. I knew this because I accompanied Regina there for a pool party earlier in the summer. I didn't really mind since it was on the way and the trip would give me some time to think about how I would explain Regina's tirade to my grandmother and my dad who I was sure already had heard about what happened. I took a left into Jessica's friend's cove and pulled up into the empty driveway. Jessica asked me if I wanted to come inside with her. I had no reason to and thought the request was odd, but her friend was attractive, so it gave me an excuse to see if she was inside maybe wearing something tight (or maybe nothing at all) not expecting a guy to be around.

Jessica walked around to the back of the house ahead of me and disappeared behind the brick. As I started to turn the corner, I saw a figure in the corner of my eye coming from around the backyard racing towards me. It was Regina. She was barreling towards me screaming curse words with two 8-inch butcher knives, one in each hand. Reflexively, I jumped back away from the slashes unscathed and sprinted towards my car. She moved much slower than me, so I knew she wouldn't catch me if I really ran but I didn't want to leave my car. I tried to open the door, but it would have been a perilous mistake with her so closely behind me, so I darted into the front lawn and took off around the corner with my heart racing. She had given up pursuit and was now sitting in the driver seat of my car with one knife in her left hand and the other knife out of eyesight. After my adrenaline returned to normal, I remembered that I was only walking distance from my house and started up the street towards my neighborhood. As soon as I turned the corner, I noticed my father's Nissan 280z driving slowly in the opposite direction. He spotted me and looked puzzled as to why I was walking.

"Where the hell is your car?" he said.

After only a few minutes of explaining what happened, my dad was pulling into Jessica's friend's driveway behind my car where

Regina remained seated. She recognized my father's car and jumped out of the driver's seat. My father threatened her with a few choice words and she gave up her position allowing me to walk towards my car. While approaching the driver's seat, I could hear the advancing sound of police sirens. Apparently, the neighbors had observed the incident and had called the police. A white Chevrolet Impala with Memphis Police Department decals and flashing lights approached. A white man with a buzz-cut and sunglasses climbed out of the driver's seat as his partner, a black female officer, opened the passenger door. Regina, Jessica and Jessica's friend Marshawn stood outside in semi-circle under the carport. I was sure that this would take a turn for the worse. Even though Regina unexplainably still had the knives in her hands, I figured the three of them would lie for her and say that I started the incident or worse had attacked Regina. Instead, Regina broke down and confessed.

"He broke up with me for no reason! You just don't understand. I'm tired of being hurt. I wasn't going to cut him, I promise," she cried.

The officers could tell that this was just another teenage drama story gone wrong and judging from their body language they weren't inclined to make an arrest.

"Young man, do you really want to press charges against this girl?" said the female officer in a sarcastic tone.

For a moment, there was complete silence. I was angry, embarrassed, sweaty, and tired.

I looked at Regina's face which was red with tears and I shook my head.

"I just want her to leave me alone and go home," I said.

The officers and my dad watched as I got into my car and backed out of the driveway. Tennessee, unlike Washington, D.C., did not require an arrest in all domestic violence cases and so the police used their discretion that day and let Regina go home after she returned the knives to the kitchen. I returned home and told my grandmother what happened. The story upset her to tears as I sat with my head in my arms thinking about how close I came to losing my life.

Difficult Decisions

I snapped out of my nostalgia and got on the phone to connect Michelle with one of our most capable advocates. Vicky was a seasoned counselor who had overcome her own personal experience with domestic violence and dedicated her career to assisting victims of domestic violence for over fifteen years. Her authentic and blunt approach with adults yet gentle and maternal connection with children helped her build trust with victims rapidly, a crucial skill for domestic violence counselors.

When we met with Michelle and Tiana for the first time, it was evident that they had been subjected to continued abuse at the defendant's hands. Michelle described a history of attacks, most of which stemmed from the defendant's unfounded suspicions of Michelle's infidelity. On the night in question, the defendant had taken Michelle's cell phone and searched through it looking for text messages from another man. Michelle tried to ignore his possessiveness and got into the bed hoping that he would join her and go to sleep. Instead, he began to put a pillow over Michelle's head and put his hand around her neck trying to choke her. Michelle fought him off and went into the living room where she picked up a hammer to defend herself, but the defendant overpowered her and took the hammer from her.

By now, Tiana had heard the commotion from her room and had already dialed police—this was not the first time that she had done so. The defendant placed the hammer to Michelle's head while Tiana watched. He threatened to bash her head in, but Michelle reached for her pepper spray sitting on the nearby counter and sprayed the defendant in the eyes causing him to flee the scene before the police arrived. Michelle recounted other occasions where she received black eyes and bruises but never called police.

I began to rethink my case value system as she told her story. How many cases had I ignored because, on the surface, they appeared too common or unimportant? During our meeting, Tiana barely made eye contact with me as she colored in a coloring book we provided for her visit. She was a beautiful little girl who seemed mature beyond her years. I explained to her the process and what it meant to testify on the stand—it would mean telling her story in her father's presence. With each question, she calmly agreed that she understood and was willing to cooperate. Tiana then told me her version of the story which matched Michelle's. I began to see my younger self in Tiana and Michelle. Tiana felt anger towards her parents for not protecting her and tried to convey a sense of fearlessness. Fear was a sign of weakness and she knew that in her environment, the weak were soon victims. Michelle felt betrayed by someone she used to love. Thinking about how Tianna must have felt began to make me angry. I hadn't sent the plea offer to the defendant's attorney yet, but I was strongly considering not sending one at all and simply adding charges based on the new information.

I also began to think about my parent's actions that night in my dad's truck. Despite their rage, I knew my mother and father were good people. They both loved me and my brother and generally treated people fairly and with respect. In that moment, their tempers simply got the best of them. Yet, had either of them called the police that night, I might have been in the same position as Tiana with the dreaded prospect of being forced to take the stand against my parents in a criminal case. What about my experience with Regina? Much later in life, we became Facebook friends and I used to check up on her from time to time. She ended up moving to North Carolina and finishing school. She currently has a thriving career and life of her own. Would the result have been the same had I decided to press charges against her that day? Likewise, was it in the best interest of Tiana to have her father spend thirty days in jail? Would he really learn a lesson or become even more hardened after being caged up with violent criminals all day?

After taking a closer look at his arrest report, it appeared that he struggled with mental health disorders for which he took no medication. These circumstances were far from an excuse for his behavior, but it provided an explanation that made me rethink my approach. I decided that prison was not the solution. I would ask for a long period of probation and a stay away order so that Michelle and Tiana could live in peace. James would receive mental health treatment through the court's supervision and perhaps would have an opportunity at redemption much like my mother and father had when I got older.

The Reckoning

It was 9:00 a.m. and the domestic violence courtroom was filled as usual. The judge hadn't taken the bench, and I was looking for my victims. When I opened the wooden door, I looked around. To the right, in the back row, sat an elderly man speaking to his defense attorney about his case. To the left, in the second to last row of seats, sat Michelle and Tiana waiving in my direction. I felt relieved to see them there, but also afraid Michelle might fold at the prospect of confronting James in court. Quite the contrary, Michelle seemed eager to see the process to the end and appeared emboldened by my presence.

"Mr. Jackson, when are they going to call our case? Do you think he will go to jail?" asked Michelle.

"Remember Michelle, I'm asking for probation, but the judge can do whatever he thinks is appropriate. I don't think he will do time but there is no way to know," I stated.

Tiana appeared stoned faced as usual. No emotions flowed from her brown eyes as she rocked back and forth in her seat reading a book while I spoke to her mom. The courtroom had started to swell with a mix of people: defendants, victims, attorneys, marshals and finally the judge. A faint double knock behind the faux-wooden backdrop signaled everyone to rise to their feet as the clerk announced the judge's presence. The judge was a small Latino middle-aged man who had been on bench for over two decades. He was notoriously defense friendly and almost never sentenced anyone to jail time. I had tried two cases in front of him and won them both and watched both of my defendants walk out of the courtroom with time served. He had been on the domestic violence rotation for over a year and you could tell he was ready to move on. The back and forth between the parties often made him pinch his forehead in frustration and lash out at either side for presenting silly arguments or attending hearings unprepared.

The clerk finally called our case.

"State your names for the record," said the judge.

"Martinis Jackson, for the government your honor," I stated.

"Jim Jones for the defense your honor," stated the defense.

I looked over at the defendant from the corner of my eye. I had expected him to come forward with his attorney but surprisingly enough, his client came from the holding cell in the back and was dressed in an orange jumpsuit. I discovered that the court had ordered him detained for violating a condition of his release by not reporting to pre-trial supervision and failing to charge his GPS monitoring device. I looked over my shoulder to glance at Tianna and Michelle and watched as they both stared angrily at the defendant. It was the first time that I saw Tianna's face exhibit any emotions. She looked angry and sad all at once.

I made my sentencing recommendation to the judge. I started by explaining the history of violence that both victims had suffered at the hands of the defendant. I made what I felt was a poignant statement to the defendant through the court that although I was not seeking jail time that I wanted the lengthiest sentence possible to hang over James' head to be triggered by the slightest violation of probation. I glanced over at my two victims again after I finished, and the defense attorney began to advocate for his client. I could see Michelle's posture change: she was sitting straight up with her head held high looking as fearless as I had ever seen her. She had her right arm wrapped tightly around Tianna's shoulder while she listened to the defense attorney make his arguments. I faced forward and looked down at my notes while occasionally glancing at the judge to see his facial expressions during defense allocution. The defense attorney wanted probation as well but sought a much shorter sentence. The defense argued that his client's action reflected an anomaly despite my belief that the assault represented only a sample of a broader cycle of violence. The defense attorney continued by blaming his client's action on drunkenness and unemployment. The excuses went on for another ten minutes. Eventually, the defense rested, and the judge finally spoke.

"Sir, would you like to say anything on your own behalf before I sentence you?" the judge asked.

"No, your honor," said the defendant.

"Your honor, I failed to mention that the victim is actually in the courtroom and forgot to ask if she actually wanted to come forward and speak," I butted in.

My comment irritated the judge. He stared at me for more than a few seconds without saying anything before responding.

"Well counsel, where is she?" he said in a sharp tone.

I pointed her out not knowing if she would simply decline or step forward.

"Yes, your honor. I would like to speak," said Michelle.

The audience all turned around to put a face with the assertive voice in the back of the courtroom. She stood up and moved past Tianna who remained seated watching her mother walk to the stand next to me at the prosecution's bench.

"Good morning ma'am, would you state your name for the record," the judge asked.

"Michelle Davis," she said.

"Is there anything you would like to say before I sentence this young man?" he said.

She paused for a second to gather her thoughts. I had my hands rested on the table with my head staring down at the desk pondering what she might say.

"Your honor, these past few weeks have been a blessing for me and my daughter," Michelle explained. "We haven't heard from James. We have lived without looking over our shoulders and wondering when he is going to pop up. This is the first time in a long time I've been able to sleep in a bed with no one yelling at me before I lay down or when I wake up. I just want it to stay that way. I honestly don't want to see him go to jail even though he probably deserves to, that's the father of my child, but I don't want him around me anymore. I'm done with him."

The spiel lasted only a few seconds but Michelle's sincerity and Tianna's presence in the courtroom was statement enough.

"Thank you, Ms. Davis. Anything else?" he said.

"No, your honor," she stated.

Michelle turned towards me and nodded her head satisfied that she had been given the opportunity to provide her input and had finally taken a stand against James. The judge stared down at his notes and slowly looked up at the defendant.

"Mr. Kemp, are you ready to be sentenced?" stated the judge.

"Yes, your honor," he said with his eyes towards the floor.

"It is clear that you have caused Ms. Davis a great deal of grief. What's more troubling is your total disregard for the safety and psychological well-being of your own daughter. Although this is your first offense, it shows that you are a danger to the community, specifically Ms. Davis and her daughter. I believe a split sentence is appropriate in this case."

When I heard the words split sentence, I did my best to conceal my confusion.

"I sentence you to 180 days of incarceration with 120 of those days suspended followed by a year of probation," stated the judge. "You must stay away from Ms. Davis and your daughter. You must participate in mental health treatment and the domestic violent intervention program. You will need to pay $50 to the victims of violent crimes fund."

Within seconds, James was marshaled back into the holding cell to spend two months in prison. I wasn't sure that Michelle understood what the sentence meant, so I walked with her and Tianna out into the hallway and explained that James would be spending some time in prison. Michelle exhaled a sigh of relief and gave me a warm hug. I was surprised she wasn't upset with the result.

"I have two more months that I don't need to worry about him. I can save up and move like I've been trying to do for the longest. Thank you again Mr. Jackson," she said smiling.

I watched as she and Tianna walked away. I hoped it would be the last time I saw them under those circumstances and frankly I figured it would be the last time I would see them ever. I wondered what their futures would hold. The system would keep James away from them for at least a year, but would it last? Would prison serve as a wake-up call for Tianna's father or would the system turn him even more violent than when he entered?

I realized how lucky I was that my parents decided to part ways. I knew it could have easily been one of them in that courtroom standing in front of the judge awaiting sentencing. Instead, they avoided a criminal record and lived productive lives raising me and my brother.

3

IT'S YOUR WORD, AGAINST MINE

Alkana was entering her sophomore year of college at a local university in Washington, D.C. She had recently transferred from an out-of-state school in hopes of starting over after a disappointing freshman experience where she struggled to balance academics and athletics. Alkana's basketball prowess earned her a full scholarship that now stood in jeopardy based on her poor performance off the court. In her freshman summer, she decided to transfer to a college that she initially rebuffed out of high school but who recruited her heavily throughout her prep career.

Prior to entering her fall semester, she attended summer classes at her new school and met Simon, a brilliant Nigerian medical student. The two became acquainted in a statistics class that Simon decided to take to assist him in writing a book he planned to author after he completed medical school. The two formed a study group with other classmates and exchanged numbers as a result. Alkana struggled in the class and often reached out to Simon for advice. On one occasion during the summer,

Simon reached out to Alkana about having lunch, but the plans fell through and the two never met outside of the summer class. Aside from their academic discussions, Simon and Alkana would also discuss Nigerian politics and their plans after graduation. Simon wanted to start his own practice in the states; Alkana wanted to return to Nigeria and become a social worker in impoverished communities. She often criticized Simon for not having in his plans to return to Nigeria where the country could use more talented doctors.

When summer classes were over, the two did not communicate again until fall semester. In September, Simon spotted Alkana on campus wearing her basketball uniform headed to practice. He sent her a text message that day asking if he could stop by her dorm room later. Alkana was surprised to see the text and responded by giving Simon permission to text her later about it.

Later that night, Alkana attended an on-campus party with her teammates and had a few drinks. At 5'5 117 lbs., it didn't take long for the alcohol to take its toll and within a few hours she was tipsy. Around 2:00 a.m., she headed back to her dorm slightly intoxicated and disoriented. She walked alone through campus until she finally made it to her building. She unlocked the door to a shared living space and headed to her bedroom and closed the door. She began to drift off to sleep when she heard her cell phone ring and saw Simon's name appear on the caller ID.

"Hey, you still awake?" he said.

"Umm…yeah, why what's up?" said Alkana.

"I'm outside your building, can I come up?" he said.

"Wait, what? Ummm, sure, I guess," she said.

Still groggy, she fell back into her bed for five minutes before she heard a knock at her front door. When she opened the door, it was Simon standing in the threshold with a backpack, a stack of red cups in his hand, and a wide smile.

A year later, Alkana was in my office explaining what happened that night after Simon entered her room.

"First we started to talk about school. I thought it was weird that he had come over so late, but I didn't want to be rude and tell him to leave. We started discussing politics and Nigeria like we always do and that's when he asked if I wanted something to drink. At first, I told him no but he insisted so I took a few sips," she stated.

"What happened next?" I said.

Alkana had told this story several times: first to the school's Title IX representative, then to the police, then to the prosecutor who had the case before me, and now to me. She described the incident as if it had happened last night as opposed to over a year ago.

"He asked me to come sit in his lap. I thought to myself 'Ok, this is weird' but I went over and sat in his lap anyway. He was so much bigger than me and after a while he started touching on my thighs. I moved his hand but he continued touching my thigh. He would say 'You know I'm much stronger than you right? I could just toss you.'"

"Why did you go sit in his lap if you didn't want to?" I asked.

"I didn't want to be mean to him and I figured he would eventually leave, if I did what he asked," Alkana said. "I was afraid that I would be raped if I yelled or fought back."

I listened as she described the hours of fondling she endured. Her story was that Simon continued his sexual assault throughout the night despite her continued requests that he refrain from touching her and leave. At one point, Simon allegedly went under her shirt and touched her breast against her will. He picked her up and held her up against the wall pressing his face against hers. When he threw her down on the bed and tugged at her underwear, she was sure she would be raped but eventually he gave up and left.

After Simon left, Alkana tried to call her closest friend who lived in California, but he was out partying and didn't pick up. She persisted that she hadn't screamed because she was sure it would turn the situation violent as Simon's 6'3 muscular frame could have easily overpowered hers. She decided not to say anything that night and went to sleep. The next day she explained what happened to her roommate and mustered up enough strength to report what happened to the school's Title IX representative who took a videotaped statement.

"That night, why didn't you call out for help from your roommate after Simon left?" I asked.

"I didn't think she was in her room, because her door was closed and usually she plays music when she sleeps. Later, I learned that she was asleep in her room the entire time. I was just relieved I didn't get raped."

She stared at me defensively with her arms folded, so I pivoted to another topic even though I had begun to develop mixed feelings about the case. Alkana gave me no reason to discredit her story, but my mind was filled with questions that I knew any good defense attorney would ask. Why had she let Simon into her room so late at night? Why would she drink his alcohol and sit in his lap if she didn't want him there? If she really thought she was about to be raped, why didn't she scream for help or run out of the room? It was clear why this case was going to trial. Simon had everything to lose and nothing to gain by pleading guilty to misdemeanor sexual assault. He had no criminal record and could take the stand to give his version of the events with no other evidence aside from my victim's own testimony. If Simon didn't come across as a complete liar and denied wrongdoing, his testimony alone would create reasonable doubt. I spent several days attempting to devise a winning strategy for the case. I came to realize that unlike other one-witness cases that I had taken to trial, this one had one advantage: Alkana's credibility. She was educated, articulate, and attractive. I wouldn't need to ask leading questions to get her to elaborate about what happened and her innocent soft voice would convince anyone she was telling the truth.

Every trial has a theme. I decided that in this case lack of motive would be the theme. Defense attorneys frequently used this theme to establish reasonable doubt, but the strategy also made sense for my case. I knew that if Alkana came across to the judge as credible as I thought she would, then only one question remained: what motivation did she have to create this detailed story about what happened to her that night? I couldn't find one and unless the defense had an explanation for why Alkana would perjure herself to put an innocent man in prison, we could possibly win.

The night before trial I was lying in my bed reflecting on Alkana's story and I wondered if there was a possibility that it was fabricated. Although securing a conviction was far from guaranteed, my confidence about our chances of winning increased. Despite my new-found assurance, I cringed at the idea that Simon's future hinged on the testimony of one woman. I kept thinking about Simon's recorded conversation with police the day after the incident. The detective called him about coming in to talk about what happened. Simon sounded the way I imagine I would have if I were being accused of sexual assault: frightened and confused. At first, he vaguely remembered being in Alkana's bedroom that night and then admitted to being there but stated that nothing had happened. I kept hearing his voice over and over again in my head.

"Sir, why would I assault someone?" he said. "I am a few months from becoming a doctor. Sir, I did not assault anyone. This is crazy."

I contemplated the number of women I had been alone with at night who, for whatever reason, could have claimed assault against me leaving a jury of my peers or a judge to decide my fate. I thought about the story of a close college friend who was a standout football player in high school. His senior year a young girl, who had allegedly slept with several members of the football team (all at once), made allegations that my friend had assaulted her. The police arrested him on serious charges of sexual assault, but my friend maintained his innocence and stated that he had no physical contact with the young girl and had no idea why she targeted him. Luckily for my friend, the young girl's story began to unravel, and the prosecutor dropped the case based on her lack of credibility, but not before admonishing my friend never again to step foot on the courthouse steps. It served as a wake-up call to my friend, who is now a highly successful business man with a family. He often recounts how quickly his life could have changed based on the false accusations of one person. I woke up the next morning with the trial at the forefront of my thoughts. I couldn't shake the idea of trying this case with so many doubts in my own mind. I washed up, put on my suit and headed out of the door for a long commute to the courthouse. On the train ride to work, I began to reflect on whether or not my doubts were based on the facts of the case or my own preconceived notions about women.

Manly Views

My views on women have continually evolved over the course of my life. Expectedly, my initial feelings were shaped by my interactions with the women who were closest to me. From infancy to my teenage years, I lived in households with no fewer than five family members residing therein. For the most part, the core group of my grandmother, father, two aunts, two uncles, and several cousins comprised the members of my home. My mother and father separated very early in my life and I had very little interaction with my mother as an adolescent. Over the years, members of my household would come and go as life led them in different directions, but my interaction with each of them developed my notions about gender norms. Specifically, my two aunts and grandmother each conveyed to me two qualities of black women that I came to admire: they worked hard, and they loved their families.

My grandmother was an immensely talented woman who was well read and held strong religious convictions. She was an amazing cook and an expert at sewing clothes, quilts, and virtually anything that a person could make using a needle, thread, and cloth. She married my grandfather at a young age and had six children. My grandfather was a tall dark-skinned man with a deep voice. He drove trucks for a living and owned a small shotgun house in Memphis' Orange Mound community. I can remember being a very young boy and visiting my grandfather on weekends. He was always excited to see me and often talked about how I would one day play in the NBA despite my miniature stature. We would watch *Bonanza* and John Wayne films together on his black and white television and he would often let me take home a jar of coins and penny wrappers when my father came to pick me up. By this point though, my grandmother had long ended the marriage between them. She had grown tired of the physical and psychological abuse that she often endured during their time together. I had heard stories of the harshness of my grandfather and saw glimpses of him in my own dad at times, but my overall experience with him was positive and somehow, me and my older cousin brought out a softer side in him. After my grandmother ended the relationship with my grandfather, she never remarried and spent most of her life earning a living by working inside the homes of wealthy white families in Memphis' affluent Chickasaw-Gardens community. Every morning she would leave our home at 5:00 a.m. and return in the evening visibly drained from a day of cooking, cleaning and caring for others. Although physically and mentally taxing, the profession paid well especially during the economic boom of the 90s which created a higher demand for her services. Most of her hard-earned money went towards caring for her family. When I was born, she encouraged my father to raise me in their household as she believed it would offer me the best chance of succeeding. She made sure I had the things I needed when my father was out of work or disinterested. Until this day, she is the most loving woman I've known and despite the many spankings I received at her hands up until I was a teenager, I credit much of my success to her.

My grandmother had two daughters. One was her oldest child and the other was the fourth of her six kids. My oldest auntie excelled in school and was the first of my grandmother's children to finish college. She majored in business and started her career at the biggest corporation in Memphis, Federal Express. She had gotten into a serious relationship during her late twenties and became pregnant with my older cousin but unfortunately the relationship didn't last, and she soon became a single mother. During my adolescence, my oldest aunt was one of my strongest mother figures in the absence of my own. She took my cousin and me to fun places and introduced us to the church. She often orchestrated Christmas and birthday celebrations making both of us feel as special as any kid could have asked to feel. She taught me about compassion and patience. Of the women in my family, she was the least likely to punish me and often reassured me that I would be great in life even in my moments of doubt.

My youngest aunt was what some might consider a tomboy growing up. She was less interested in dresses and getting married than she was playing competitive games or going fishing. She decided to join the Air Force out of high school and spent much of her time traveling the world. My father and I lived with my aunt when she was stationed in Oklahoma for a short while before she eventually moved back to Memphis. She was loving and always had a great sense of humor, but I learned quickly that if you got on her bad side she could be as aggressive as any man I knew. I will never forget the time she came up to my elementary school to confront the administration for using corporal punishment against me more regularly than other offending white students my age. She stormed into the principal's office and told them that this was the last time they would use the paddle on me; I was never paddled again. Ironically, when I got home I received a beating worse than the ones I had gotten at school for my behavior, but even at the age of ten I understood the difference between tough love and hate. When she returned home permanently from the Air Force, she eventually landed a job at the post office working the night shift. She dreaded the work, but endured the gruesome schedule, physical demands, and monotony to provide for my two younger cousins that she birthed while in her early thirties.

Each of the women in my life were caring, hardworking, and humble. They weren't overly concerned with their appearances or materialistic values. As I matured, I noticed that the women in my life were a lot like the women in many of my childhood friend's lives. Almost all of them went to work every day with the sole purpose of providing a better life for their children.

Unfortunately, as I grew older, my experiences at home began to compete with the images portrayed through mainstream media and social interaction. I began to assimilate into a culture that viewed women as objects whose purpose was primarily for the enjoyment of men. The message from much of mainstream media was that women were not to be trusted or placed on a pedestal, such conduct was a sign of weakness in a man. In the 90s, I began listening to the likes of Sir Mix-a-lot, Two Live Crew, and Too Short as they described their graphic exploits of women. Three-6 mafia was my favorite local group and was notorious for their demeaning lyrics about women. The lyrics echoed in the hallways off of the tongues of myself and many of my classmates. Kids who couldn't tell you the elements on the periodic table could remember an entire rap album in a week's time. Music videos with half-naked dancers were broadcast in the 90s and served as prime entertainment for teenagers (including myself) just beginning to develop a sexual identity. Of course, it wasn't simply rap music and videos, shows on networks such as HBO and Cinemax provided access to R and X-rated movies that reinforced the objectification of women. I often found myself conflicted between the positive examples of women at home and the negative stereotypes cast in the media.

Like many of my friends, very little of what went into my mind was censored by adults. I am convinced that the apparent neglect wasn't so much that parents were irresponsible or apathetic; they either didn't have the time to monitor their child's every step or failed to grasp the impact that the media was having on their offspring. Others were just as much a product of the culture as their children and saw nothing wrong with the exposure. Besides, even the strictest parent couldn't prevent his or her child from going to school and borrowing a Walkman from a classmate to listen to the latest music or heading over after school to watch the latest video.

The more I reflected on my middle school and high school experiences, the more I wondered how significant an impact mainstream media had on students' sexual identities and relationship values. Certainly, adolescent sexual experimentation was not a new phenomenon, but I wondered how closely the actions of my peers reflected real life emulating entertainment as opposed to innocent exploration. For instance, it was common place in my middle school to see young boys and girls twelve years old and younger attending school dances with highly sexual behaviors on display, many of the dances were mirror images of what you would find on rap music videos. As you can imagine, these school dances did very little to instill in young boys a level of respect for young girls who often drew attention not by way of their personalities but by dancing as provocatively as possible with as many boys as possible.

Even horseplay between genders was rarely innocent, many of my male associates thought it normal to chase down young girls and grope and grab them for fun. For the girls, three choices existed in response to this behavior: acceptance, retaliation, or telling a teacher. Very few chose the latter two options as it appeared many of them had grown accustomed to the treatment. The teachers did little to intervene. They often had too many students to monitor and were more concerned with fighting between students than this seemingly playful contact. When teachers did respond, they did so by directing boys to timeout or at most sending them to the office where they often returned after a warning. The girls would rarely receive an apology and were often told not to worry about it and to continue playing. This response reinforced the idea that pursuit of girls meant aggressive behavior focused on physical contact as opposed to building a healthy friendship by engaging in conversation.

In high school, the behavior graduated from provocative dancing and horseplay to outright sexual activity. Young girls with fully-developed bodies started to draw even more attention from their male classmates. For many of the girls who were shy in middle school, the newfound interest from boys boosted their self-esteem making them feel desirable and attractive. High school boys treated virginity as a badge of shame that they hoped no-one would discover. As a result, many either lied about their exploits or prepared to endure continued verbal abuse from their peers. Add the biological impulses already at work in teenagers to a conservative southern culture that virtually prohibited sex education and there is no wonder pregnancy was a common occurrence in my high school.

I observed the objectification of women continue into college. However, at this point, my friends and I could no longer use ignorance as an excuse. We were aware of the racist agendas of powerful groups that used the media as a tool to further its goals. Images and words associated with African Americans portrayed us as violent, unintelligent, athletic and/or promiscuous. Nevertheless, some of us continued to use demeaning language in our discussions about women and treat them as play toys ready to be enjoyed and discarded whimsically. Luckily, as I got older and wiser, I began to understand the hypocrisy underlying my treatment of women. I hated racism, yet my sexist behavior played right into the hands of those who rely on division and self-hatred in the black community to perpetuate stereotypes and systemic racism.

It was through this lens that I prosecuted sex offenses. I started to think about Alkana's case differently. Maybe her actions were justified that night; no one would have questioned her silent acquiescence to a robber's demands. But since the case involved sexual contact with a person she knew, she would be questioned at every turn about her failure to fight back. Clearly, she should have expected some aggressiveness from Simon that night. Obviously, the entire situation was her fault for inviting him in so late and having a drink with him. What woman would do all these things and not want to have sex? If she didn't want to be touched, she should have fought with all her might, right? I realized that I had no reason to question her story aside from my own prejudices towards women and preconceived notions about sexual interaction. I thought back to middle school and all those girls who were conditioned to endure abuse silently.

The Moment of Truth

During trial, Alkana came across as credible as any witness I had ever put on the stand. The level of detail with which she described Simon's actions was incredibly persuasive. She even recounted the specifics of their conversation that night. Simon was upset about his mother's recent surgery and showed Alkana pictures on his phone of his mother in the hospital. This fact was supported by Simon's recorded conversation with police when he mentioned his mother's recent surgery, which explained why he might have been drinking heavily that night. Alkana's answers did not appear rehearsed and she admitted when she couldn't remember a specific detail. During cross-examination, she handled the defense attorney's probing questions with stoicism, refraining from becoming defensive.

When she stepped down from the stand, I felt ashamed that I had doubted her story. I called as my next witness the Title IX representative who recorded Alkana's statement. Her role was to reinforce Alkana's story. Typically, her testimony would have been inadmissible hearsay, but in sexual assault cases the court allows such hearsay to avoid an inference that the victim failed to report, which in turn could lead to a false assumption that no assault occurred. In a bench trial (where the judge determines the verdict and not the jury), this was less relevant because the judge was less likely to make such assumptions. The additional testimony simply served to bolster Alkana's claim by showing that she made consistent statements close in time to the incident. When she was finished, I rested my case and it was the defense's turn.

Simon decided to take the stand, which suggested that our case was strong enough to force him to tell his story. He stood up from the defense table in a navy-blue tailored suit. He was tall and dark-skinned wearing chic black prescription glasses. He walked to the witness stand with his hands in the pockets while taking long strides towards the wooden box. His attorney began and ended his questioning rather quickly. Simon gave very short answers and came across as awkward on the stand. Clearly, the two had not rehearsed his testimony as the defense attorney drew several sustained objections for asking leading questions. Simon gave the same account he had given police a few days after the incident. He had gone over to Alkana's dorm room to hang out. When he arrived, they had a few drinks together and started to play music from his phone, but it began to annoy Alkana so he left. He said that he never once touched her and that he remained in Alkana's room for no more than fifteen minutes. I cross-examined him briefly, but there wasn't much I could do with his version. I expected Simon to admit to touching Alkana but state the touching was consensual or that Alkana was the one who seduced him. I asked a few questions on cross and took a seat. During closing statements, I beat the judge over the head with my theme. I repeated the word "motive" at least ten times during my speech.

"Your honor, where is the motive for this young woman to take the stand under penalty of perjury and lie about what happened that night?" I asked. "The two barely knew each other well enough for her to develop that type of hatred for him. Why would she go through the trouble of reporting this to her friends, family, school, police, and in open court just to get this young man in trouble?"

The defense attorney did his best to soften the blow.

"Your honor, if we convict this young man, we are saying that as long as the court can't find a motive for a young woman to lie about a sexual assault then the court can convict based solely on the testimony of one witness," he said.

The statement struck a nerve with me and I was sure it hit home with the judge. Not surprisingly, the judge needed more time to decide and told us to return later in the day for his verdict.

Alkana and her parents awaited outside with questions about my expectations. I assured them that we had put on the best case that we could and that regardless of the outcome, Alkana had told the truth and had her day in court. They were satisfied with my response and left the courthouse to have lunch while awaiting the verdict.

I returned to the empty courtroom early to clear my mind before the verdict. I was reflecting on my presentation of the case, critiquing every decision. I should have asked more questions; I should have introduced more text messages. Why hadn't I spent enough time cross-examining the defendant? Eventually, the lunch break ended, and my thoughts were cut short. The courtroom fell silent as the judge appeared from his chambers. He sat down and asked that we be seated while he walked us through his decision. Typically, in bench trials, the judge reviews the testimony and explains which party's version of events she believes (i.e. credits). Our judge read through his notes regarding Alkana's testimony and credited all of it. This was certainly good news for my case, but it didn't necessarily mean we had won. If by some strange chance the judge credited Simon's testimony as well, we would be out of luck.

"Now, as for the defendant's story," said the judge. "I simply cannot credit his testimony that he went over to the victim's home that night with no intentions at all. It makes no sense that he would go all the way over to her bedroom at 2:00 a.m. with a bottle of liquor and leave after fifteen minutes. After observing his testimony and demeanor while testifying, I do not credit his testimony."

Simon stared at the judge with a look of horror as he continued his speech. Anyone in the courtroom who was paying attention knew the verdict at this point; the rest was a mere formality. When he finished I could see the defense attorney trying to calm Simon down, drawing him close whispering words into his ear. Alkana, her father and mother were the only other people in the audience and they appeared relieved when they heard the verdict. Simon on the other hand was appalled. At times he looked as if he would cry and others as if he wanted to charge the bench. When the judge set the sentencing date, Simon darted out of the courtroom fuming with anger. I walked towards the door happy the trial was finally over and spoke with Alkana about sentencing. She looked as if an immense weight had been lifted off her shoulders. It was the first time I saw her smile throughout the several months that we saw each other. The judge would later sentence Simon to only a few days in jail but the collateral consequences of having a misdemeanor sexual assault charge on his record were much more severe: he would need to disclose his conviction before seeking his license as a physician. It came as no surprise that he immediately appealed the decision. Despite hiring one of the most expensive lawyers in town to replace his attorney, he lost the appeal.

Alkana finally had closure. She often called and thanked me for helping her with the case which lasted over a year during the appeal process. After we parted ways, I thought about how conflicted I felt. Thoughts of the many women I encountered in my life (family, friends, and lovers) raced through my head. Many of them had their own stories of sexual assault that never made it to court. Some of them were victimized at too young an age to realize it was wrong at the time, others were simply too afraid to come forward. I felt that they would have been proud of what I had accomplished for Alkana. I realized the important role that reflecting on my own life experiences with women played; the process not only helped me empathize with Alkana's situation, but also forced me to challenge my own assumptions about sexual assault. On the other hand, when I watched Simon storm out of the courtroom disgusted with the system, I could not help but think about the men I knew who had been falsely accused of a crime (including myself) with no way of proving they hadn't committed it or whose actions were a result of years of being socialized to believe that what a woman really means when she says "no" is "convince me". Seeing both sides was truly a gift and a curse.

4

SO YOU THINK YOU'RE A LAWYER, HUH?

"Bro, this was an epic night! These junts in Orlando fine as hell. Shit was a good ass time, bruh," said Tariq.

"Hell, yeah, man, I definitely could live here bro," I said.

We were both sitting inside of a Chevrolet Caprice that was parked in a parking garage in downtown Orlando. A group of four girls that we met inside of a local club dropped us off at our car. Tariq's consumption of Coronas had taken its toll, so I became the designated driver. It was my first time in Orange County and I had no idea where we were, so I entered Tariq's father's address in the GPS before I turned out of the parking garage and headed towards the interstate. I took a left turn out of the garage and followed the digital path on the screen. I drove a few miles before making another right onto a dark street that led to the highway. Immediately after making the right turn, Tariq and I heard the distinct sound of emergency response sirens. Instinctively, I pulled over to the right of the road to allow the vehicle to pass. Oddly, the sirens and flashing lights persisted as I came to a complete stop. Tariq did a nervous turnaround in the passenger seat to glance at the police car that had pulled behind us.

"I know I wasn't speeding. Did you have your seatbelt on?" I said.

"Yea man, seatbelt is right here," said Tariq as he pointed as his buckles.

I remained calm and glanced at my rearview mirror to observe two officers approaching the car. A middle aged white man with a military style haircut approached the driver's side with a flashlight in his left hand, and his right hand close to his holster.

My window was already half-way down and I noticed, in my rearview, the other officer examining my license plates with his own flashlight while his partner continued towards my window. I was driving a rental car, but I had my documents in the glove compartment. I knew we didn't have anything illegal in the car, so I figured this would be a brief encounter.

"Sir, you do realize that you were swerving in the street back there," the officer said.

"I don't recall swerving." I said with an incredulous tone.

"Have you had anything to drink tonight sir?" he said.

"I had two beers around 10:00 p.m.," I responded.

"Step out of the car please sir," he said.

The officer's request surprised me. I naively believed that my honest response would help to create rapport and possibly lead to our release. In hindsight, the specific answer to the question didn't matter so long as the general answer was yes. The number of beers was irrelevant, the narrative would later read "driver admitted to recently consuming alcohol". I opened the car door and stood beside the hood of the car. The officer who had approached the car asked that I participate in a field sobriety test. At this point, I was angry and sober.

"Look man, I'm not drunk. I told you I only had a few beers earlier. I wasn't swerving.

I'm a lawyer," I said.

"Sir, we are going to ask that you follow our instructions," said the white officer.

I wasn't quite a lawyer yet, but I wanted to let them know that I was educated and not some ignorant person who didn't know his rights. My statement only made them even more intent on harassing me.

His partner was silent the entire time. He was a Hispanic male in his mid to late twenties with dark gelled hair. He maintained a distance of about ten feet from us and looked poised to spring into action at the slightest hint of conflict. I wanted to refuse to cooperate, but since I knew I was sober I figured if I simply complied they would release me. The white officer pulled out a pen and asked that I follow it with my eyes while keeping my head still. Despite my compliance, I would later read the officer's report to say "failed to maintain eye contact with object". Next, the officer asked me to recite my ABC's backwards, an awkward request that I struggled to execute on a dark road in front of two strangers, with guns, eager to arrest me. Still, I slowly recited them in reverse until I was abruptly interrupted and asked to move on to the next exercise. Next, the officer commanded that I walk a straight line with my heels touching my toes while facing forward and touching my index finger to my nose. I began my walk of shame and made it to the squad car where I was told to stop. When I turned around, I could see Tariq's face through the back window staring intently at the embarrassing display. When I got to the car, the white officer gave his partner a nod and I was asked to place my hands behind my back.

"Why am I under arrest? I did everything you asked me to do," I said.

With no response, the Hispanic officer stuffed me into the back of the car pressing my head down to avoid it striking the roof of the car. I sat in the plastic back seat with metal cuffs pressed tightly against my wrists. After a fifteen-minute drive of silence, the car stopped at a satellite precinct where the police processed suspected drunk drivers. The two officers walked me into the facility and placed me in a room with a camera and a breathalyzer. They explained that I had a choice: I could take the breathalyzer and urine test, or I could refuse both and incur an automatic one-year suspension of my driver's license. I waited for a few seconds to think about it before they pressed me to decide immediately. I didn't trust the machine, but I was confident about my sobriety, so I hesitantly agreed and blew into the breathalyzer.

I wasn't fully aware of the legal limits at the time but when the test results came back with a blood alcohol level of .02. I was sure that they would release me, but I was wrong. Instead, they marshalled me into the bathroom where a clear plastic cup was sitting on top of the toilet. They placed my cuffs in front of my body and told me to fill the cup to the red line and knock on the door when I was finished. When I was done, I asked if I would be released given my breathalyzer results. I received no response to my inquiry. Instead, an officer I had never seen before escorted me to a room with one window on the door. I peeked into the window and saw five intoxicated men sprawled out on the floor of the white padded room. When I entered the room, only one of the men appeared semi-conscious, the others were asleep on the floor drunk beyond measure. The one conscious detainee was a white man who appeared to be in his late forties. He wore a nice watch and a linen suit and wreaked of alcohol. He could barely stand on his feet and his eyes circled as if he would puke at any moment. Still in shock, I stood in the corner and listened to him talk to himself for about fifteen minutes. Eventually, the man turned his attention towards me.

"Why on earth are you in here? You sure don't look drunk to me," he said with slurred speech.

"I don't know man; I have no idea," I said.

After about twenty minutes in the holding facility, the white officer who arrested me opened the door to the room and escorted us into a large van. We were handcuffed again and placed in our own seats on the van. The drive was about thirty minutes to Orange County Jail. When we arrived, I continued to ask the officer why they arrested me since I was clearly sober. As suspected, the rhe-torical question failed to appeal to the officer's logic, but that did not stop me from trying. The van entered a large electronically operated gate with barbed wire coiled at the top, and, upon entry, we parked near a large brick building. We were ushered into the building where there were several other detainees being booked for various crimes. Most of the prisoners were black; men and women were being processed in the same facility. The white officer who arrested me dropped us off and turned his back to leave.

"Wait man, why am I here? I am not drunk," I said.

He turned his back and walked out of the building and I never saw him again.

A long line awaited inside of the jail. While standing near the back of the line, I observed a man in a white tank top and baggy blue jeans standing three people in front of me complaining that he had to urinate.

"Yo, C.O. I gotta piss bad man. I need to go right now!" the man said.

"Hold it. There's a restroom in the atrium once we book you," the officer said.

"I can't bro, please!" the man said.

"You'll have to wait like everyone else," said the officer.

After about five minutes of squirming, I watched as the man's pants became discolored and a yellow liquid ran onto the floor. Those of us in line expressed our disgust by attempting to move out of the line and yelling at the guards about what was happening. None of the guards budged.

"Let him sit there in his own piss. He should have waited," said the officer.

When I finally got to the front of the line, I observed the booking process. The processor provided each inmate with prison clothes and told us to remove any belts and strings from our shoes. A guard then took each inmate's belongings and placed them in a plastic bag. I watched as one woman approached the front of the

71

line and became upset about having to take off her clothes. She was a short plump black woman in her mid-thirties who appeared familiar with the process. When she refused, a group of guards in blue uniforms began to approach her. A black male guard with a bald head and beer belly stood at the center of the group.

"You have two choices, we can do this the easy way or we can do this the hard way," said the black portly guard.

The guards began to place blue plastic gloves over their hands in anticipation of a physical encounter. The woman stood her ground and refused to comply with the guard's directives.

"Fuck yall, I'm not taking my shit off," she said.

The bald guard immediately rushed the woman tackling her to the floor as the other guards grabbed her limbs and dragged her away kicking and screaming. The woman struggled with the group jerking and pulling away from the onslaught to no avail. Her jeans were starting to fall below her waist and her back was scrubbing against the filthy floor. The other inmates watched the scene in dismay, many of them shouting their disapproval to the guards. The guards took her into a room and I never saw her again.

Eventually, I reached the front of the line. I handed the guard my belongings and put on a paper-thin, orange jumpsuit before entering the atrium where all the other inmates were sitting. The atrium was about two thousand square feet of open space with couches spread throughout the area. The processing area abutted the atrium. Near the front stood five separate booths with glass service windows. On the other side of the windows were operators who assisted inmates with placing phone calls. I walked up to one of the booths and asked the operator for help. Luckily, I knew my girlfriend's number by heart and called her. I had no idea the time, but I knew it had to be early in the morning, so I wasn't sure she would answer. To my surprise, she picked up after the third ring and sounded wide awake. Apparently, Tariq had already called her and explained what had happened. I hadn't spoken to a familiar voice in hours and felt relieved. She said she would work on getting me out as soon as possible and, after a short conversation, the operator told me that my time was up.

I started to feel better about the situation after reflecting on the temporary nature of my bondage. I sat in the atrium refusing to eat the bologna sandwich and bruised orange the jail had provided me. After about an hour, I noticed that periodically the guards would take a group from the atrium to an elevator and the group wouldn't return. The groups were separated by gender for the first time and I wasn't excited about the prospect of going to another area in the jail. After about forty minutes passed, a guard pointed to me and told me that it was time to go. The guard ushered me onto an elevator with ten other inmates and three guards. The elevator opened on the fifth floor to an open room with numerous bunkbeds, some of which were already occupied by inmates. We were directed inside and given a bunk. The room had one silver toilet in the corner near one of the bunks and a television mounted near the ceiling showing the news. It was freezing and the jumpsuits did little to combat the cold, neither did the razor thin sheets on the bed. I walked to my bunk and sat on top of the covers watching everyone around me but trying not to make eye contact. For the first time that night, I had an opportunity to reflect on how the hell I ended up in jail.

How It All Started

In the summer of 2009, I made the unexpected decision to attend law school. After three years of teaching English and coaching basketball, I was burned out from the teaching part. My passion for coaching could not overcome my frustration with overcrowded classrooms, under-resourced schools, and a lack of community support. In search of a new path, I began reading books written by successful professionals to gain inspiration and stumbled across *A Journey to Justice* written by the late Johnnie Cochran. The biography spoke about Cochran's upbringing in the south and his family's eventual move to California where he attended UCLA for undergrad and Loyola Marymount for Law School. Cochran's path as a lawyer inspired me. His journey included time as a prosecutor, and a criminal defense/civil rights attorney who focused largely on protecting the rights of African Americans. The book described Cochran's experiences fighting for clients who had been brutalized by LAPD and his own personal experiences with racism. I started to wonder what it would be like to follow in his footsteps. Like Cochran, I've always held a burning desire to fight racism and its manifestations. I was born in a city that remained largely segregated despite the Supreme Court's ruling in *Brown v. Board of Educ.* and the unraveling of *de jure* (legal) separate-but-equal. Memphis' inner city was largely African American while whites resided on the outskirts of the city in the suburbs. Many of the whites owned businesses and held decent paying jobs within the city, but, after work, they drove their cars and dollars back to their neighborhoods in the suburbs leaving Memphis as one of the poorest cities in the country. The racial animus between whites and blacks stemmed back to slavery, continued into Jim Crow, and only deepened with the assassination of Dr. Martin Luther King Jr. at the Lorraine Hotel during the Memphis Sanitation Worker Strike.

Despite the surrounding poverty, my family prospered in the late 80s and early 90s, which afforded us a nicer home in the suburbs. During this time, my older cousin and I lived in a community and attended an elementary school with a majority white population. In elementary school, I recall receiving poor marks on my report card from my teachers and being labeled a troublemaker. One teacher asked the principal to remove me from her class due to my behavior. Eventually the principal relented and placed me in another teacher's class, oddly none of my white friends who behaved similarly were ever removed. The principals paddled me with a 4-inch thick wooden paddle on a regular basis for flipping other classmates the middle finger or looking up girl's dresses on the playground. My actions certainly appeared paddle worthy except my white friends who accompanied me on these missions were spared the beatings. Somehow, I was always labeled the ring leader as if my actions inspired others to misbehave.

Eventually, the economy changed, and my family could no longer afford to live in the more affluent part of town. We moved to east Memphis in between two notorious, rival housing projects: Walter Simmons and Getwell Gardens. I immediately went from attending schools with majority white classmates to schools where African Americans comprised ninety-eight-percent of the population with sprinkles of other ethnicities here and there. Reflecting on middle and high school, my teachers served as the largest share of my interaction with other ethnicities and nationalities. Immediately, I noticed the differences between my old and new community. At my new school, I received better grades, and although I wasn't a model of good behavior, I was never suspended or asked by a teacher to transfer classes. Teachers characterized my actions as normal attention seeking behavior and not a result of an immutable character flaw. I also started to notice other more negative differences. Many of my classmates came to school hungry and showed signs of poor hygiene. Some of them struggled to read at grade level or focus in class. Fighting and violence were common occurrences. I witnessed gang fights and shootings while walking home from school. I had friends who were shot and some murdered before they graduated high school.

College reintroduced me to white America. Though I rarely experienced overt racism, I encountered subtle reminders of the clear divide between the two groups. There was the British literature professor who invited me into his office and explained to me that I wasn't cut out for college and that I should consider other options based on my performance in his class. Somehow, he interpreted my lack of enthusiasm for *Sir Gawain and the Green Knight* with an inability to succeed in college altogether; I wondered if he had done the same for my other struggling white classmates who also hated his class. Then there were days I wondered how my University's demographic could consist of less than 40 percent

African American while located in a city where African Americans made up 60 percent of the population and only a handful of colleges existed. I could recall the police coming to shut down the black student's parties, but when the white students set a couch on fire and tossed it onto the campus lawn, no sirens were to be heard. These and numerous other experiences, coupled with my own education about the plight of African Americans, motivated me to find ways to expose and change the system. Aside from this mission, the more I thought about becoming a lawyer, the more I realized how much I enjoyed many of the things lawyers did on a regular basis: reading, writing, and debating. Although I hated public speaking, I had gained immense confidence during my time as a teacher. I figured if I could withstand years of derision at the hands of ninety students a day; I could survive a courtroom with only a few people criticizing me.

The Long Road to Esquire

My first real step towards pursuing law school came with the dreaded Law School Admission Test (LSAT). The thought of becoming a lawyer wasn't new to me. I remember searching the internet, around my sophomore year of college, looking for the requirements for admittance into law school. It came as no surprise to me that having stellar undergraduate grades increased a prospect's chances of admittance. However, I also noticed that scoring high on the LSAT would significantly increase my chances of entry despite mediocre grades, an inspiring fact for a C student. I searched for LSAT questions online to get a feel for the exam and came across an online resource that offered past questions as practice. The first section dealt with logic games, which consisted of a scenario governed by several rules. Once the test taker read the fact pattern, which contained the rules of the game, they had to answer specific hypothetical questions related to the game. After about twenty minutes of frustration with the games, I made the quick decision that I wasn't cut out for law school. I would have never guessed that five years later I would again find myself considering becoming a lawyer.

Since I couldn't afford an expensive study course, I knew I would need to outwork my competition. I purchased books by Kaplan, Princeton Review, and other reputable sources I found online. For months, I spent my time reading and taking practice tests. Instead of spending my lunch break gossiping with my colleagues, I closed the door to my classroom and worked out logic games on my chalkboard. Sometimes, while the students were quiet working on assignments, I would sneak in a few LSAT questions at my desk. The more I studied, the more addictive the process became. My confidence grew with each day as I started to notice patterns in the types of questions I completed. I spent many of my weekends in the library with a former classmate and close friend, Tariq, who was also studying to take the exam.

Tariq had recently finished undergrad and wanted to attend the University of Memphis for law school. I graduated a year before him and we became friends by way of our mutual passion: basketball. We bonded after winning the annual intramural tournament while I was in graduate school and remained friends. We shared more than basketball in common; we both became fathers at a young age and wanted to provide a better life for our young sons. Tariq's experience working part time for a local real estate law firm inspired his legal pursuit. He saw the lifestyles of the partners at the firm and aspired to follow their paths, plus he enjoyed debating as much as I did and saw law as a way to exercise those skills. The two of us spent a lot of time together talking about the exam and our dreams of law school and becoming lawyers. We would camp out in the public library for hours and discuss strategies. Afterwards, we took practice exams that lasted four hours at a time. The schedule was brutal, but the reciprocal moral support made the process bearable. We studied for months leading up to the exam pushing each other to our limits in preparation for it.

When the test date finally came, I was a nervous wreck. I couldn't sleep the night before and I woke up exhausted. When I arrived at the test center, I struggled to find the right building on the large campus and panicked thinking that I would miss the test altogether. When I finally found the building, I looked up my name on the list posted on the wall and headed to my assigned classroom. I provided my signature on the sign-in sheet and sat in my wooden desk awaiting the test. My stomach was hurting, and my mind was racing. The room was freezing cold and filled with nervous silence. When the test began, the time seemed to pass much more quickly than during practice. I struggled to answer all the questions, especially on the logic games. Before I knew it, the exam was over and all I could do was leave the room and wait to see if the months of hard work would pay off.

In the interim, I began purchasing books about how to succeed in law school. I vowed to attend someone's law school, so long as it was accredited. First, I purchased the book *Planet Law School II* by Atticus Falcon. The book provided a roadmap for success in law school and explained the pedagogical malpractice that occurred at most schools. It uncovered the secrets for gaining an upper-hand on my peers before stepping foot on campus. I purchased several resources recommended by the book and credit much of my success in law school to it. After about a month of reading, my score arrived. The results weren't great, but they weren't depressing either. I knew that I could gain admittance to several schools with my score and I realized that I could probably score higher if I tried again. Tariq hadn't been so lucky. This was his third time taking the test and his score got worse and I felt I had let him down as a study partner. He congratulated me on my achievement and encouraged me to take the test again but stated that he would not retake the exam and would take his chances with his previous scores.

The second time around, I decided to change my study materials. I came across a book titled the *Logic Bible* and decided to give it a try. I put in even more hours than before, absent Tariq's encouragement. I dedicated every hour of free time to studying. When I sat for the exam in December, I was a different person. I felt like a professional athlete headed to the championship for the second time—the fear of failure had vanished. I knew I was prepared and since I already had a respectable score, I was confident that I wouldn't do any worse than before. I finished each section with time to spare and walked out self-assured.

It was February 2010, and I was already receiving acceptance letters from numerous law schools across the country based on my first score. My second score hadn't arrived yet, but I decided to start visiting the schools that accepted me. I had cast a wide net during the application process, so my travels took me all over the country to law schools located in Ohio, Alabama, Missouri, and California. In late February, I received another acceptance letter from a private law school in Orlando. Tariq was also strongly considering the school and was waiting to hear back, so we decided to visit together since his father lived about ten minutes outside of the city. With Miami only a few hours away, I now had an excuse to visit.

We arrived in Orlando on Thursday evening so that we could attend the law school event on Friday morning. When we arrived in Orlando, we ate at a local steakhouse and discussed sports and life over a bevy of beers while college basketball played in the background. It felt good to get away from teaching for a while and the weather was much nicer in Florida in February than it was in Tennessee. During our drive to the restaurant, I tried picturing myself living in Florida for three years. The weather was relatively nice year-round save the occasional tropical storm, and the cost of living mirrored Memphis'. There were no state taxes and houses were affordable. Orlando was a long distance from my family, but I could afford the law school and they were offering a scholarship. Though it was not my first choice, I wanted to keep my options open.

Friday, we visited the law school and we had the opportunity to speak with the dean of admissions as well as other enrolled students.

Everyone I spoke to was pleasant and seemed highly motivated about practicing law. The more I spoke with people, the more excited I became about the prospect of becoming a lawyer. After our visit, I left the school enthusiastic about what was to come. That night Tariq and I decided to visit downtown Orlando and get a feel for the night life. We patronized a local cigar shop and discussed the visit over drinks. The experience impressed Tariq but he still had his mind set on attending the University of Memphis. As we smoked cigars and Tariq drank bourbon, we had no idea that a few hours later I would need a lawyer of my own.

Freedom

I was laying under the covers in my bed shivering from the cold inside the large open living space with about ten men in it. Three of them were white and the rest of us were black. Part of the group that rode up with me on the elevator had gone to another part of the jail, which meant I was surrounded by even more unfamiliar faces. Some of the men were asleep in their beds, others were sitting up watching television or staring at the walls. I had never been to jail before so all I could think about was *Shawshank Redemption, Felon* and all the other prison films I had watched in my life. I just knew I would have to fight someone that night and showering, of course, was out of the question. With no clock in the cell every minute seemed like an eternity. For an hour, I thought about how easily the police had arrested me and taken me to jail. I had done nothing wrong, but it didn't matter. I was black and driving a nice car in Orange County. They used suspicion of drunk driving as a pretext for a broader search in hopes of finding something more valuable like drugs or guns. The field sobriety test was a completely subjective spectacle offering police unfettered discretion to arrest me for the slightest miscue. Even though I had passed with flying colors, the report read otherwise, even noting my apparent "insubordinate and uncooperative" behavior despite my full compliance. I thought about Cochran's experience with LAPD while driving his luxury Rolls Royce near Hollywood. A white officer ordered Cochran out of his car and harassed him in front of his children. I wondered what would have happened if Tariq wasn't a witness in the car that night; one wrong move and I might have found myself the victim of a police shooting as had Tamir Rice, Philando Castile, Michael Brown and hundreds of other young African-American men and women. The Supreme Court's interpretation of the Fourth Amendment's prohibition against unreasonable searches and seizures established a probable cause standard that police easily overcame through the guise of a traffic stop; "swerving" was all the police needed that night to stop and accuse me of drinking and driving.

Around 10:00 a.m. the next morning, my girlfriend posted my bail and the prison released me. Tariq met me behind the jail in the rental car. After my arrest, the officers had let him park the car nearby and call his father for a ride home. In the morning, Tariq's dad took him to pick up the car and then afterward Tariq waited outside of the prison for my release. I missed my flight to Memphis and had to rebook a flight for Monday. I stayed at Tariq's father's house that night and contacted a lawyer to help me fight the DUI charge. I explained to her that I wasn't drunk and that the police arrested me unlawfully. She described my options and encouraged me to enter a diversion program where I would pay the state a few thousand dollars, attend a driving class, and have the conviction expunged from my record if I completed the program successfully. She noted the severity of a DUI conviction, how it could mean a suspended driver's license, jeopardizing my future admittance to the bar, and include stiff probationary requirements. She explained that a trial would mean the officer's word against mine. This was her recommendation before she even reviewed my urinalysis or breathalyzer results. She clearly wanted to plea my case out as soon as she could and move on to other matters. I maintained my innocence and refused to agree to a plea, but she didn't believe me until my breathalyzer and urine results came back.

After my attorney reviewed my results, she spoke with the prosecutor in the case and convinced him to drop my DUI down to a traffic ticket for careless driving. I was relieved and angry at the same time. I wanted to fight the careless driving charge and bring a claim for unlawful arrest, but I didn't have the money or the time to pursue my claim. I paid the court costs and ticket and moved on with my life.

I realized what happened to me was an everyday occurrence for black people in this country, and I considered myself fortunate. For many others, racial profiling and unlawful arrests led to guilty pleas or even deadly encounters that rarely befell other racial groups. As a prosecutor, I often quizzed officers on their reasoning for stopping suspects. Sometimes the explanations didn't pass the smell test, and I did not hesitate to express my concern where I felt an officer targeted people based on their appearance or the part of town they were in as opposed to what they were doing. In some cases where I felt an officer's actions were inappropriate, I would extend favorable plea offers or look for ways to dismiss the case altogether depending on the severity of the charge. In many cases, the police were responding to legitimate criminal or suspicious activity, but, if not, I made it my duty to prevent oppressive and discriminatory patrolling when possible. In those cases, my thoughts would always return to that dark night in Florida where the false statements of one officer could have changed my life forever. Not everyone in my office shared the same views about officers' justifications for making stops. I knew some who took officers' words as gospel, and others who viewed issues surrounding initial stops as barriers to the "real" issue in the case: guilt or innocence. I knew their views were largely a consequence of never knowing the anger of being a target of racial profiling or an unlawful arrest. If I could help it, I would not reward a system whose agents abused their power at the expense of those who looked like me.

JUSTICE

"My job as a prosecutor is to do justice.
And justice is served when a guilty man is
convicted and an innocent man is not."

—SONIA SOTOMAYOR

As I began to cut my teeth as a prosecutor, I developed more realistic expectations for the criminal justice system. I discovered practical obstacles to administering justice fairly that were not going to disappear overnight, but I decided that making small corrections to a process riddled with errors was better than doing nothing at all. I learned to use my power in a way that went unnoticed by most observers but would have a significant impact on the lives of the parties involved. I was able to impose my views of fairness on the system without violating the rules that governed it, but things didn't start out that way.

Early in my career, I quickly learned that a prosecutor's discretion is constrained by the external and internal guidelines of the office. Some of these rules were created by separate bodies such as the Department of Justice, and others were established internally by the District Attorney, U.S. Attorney, and/or the supervisors within the office. Deviation from these guidelines could prove fatal to a prosecutor's career, especially if the violation backfired and became public. There are stories of prosecutors who released defendants from jail against policy. Later they had to explain that decision when the defendant was found to have committed a violent crime while on release. Another point of contention in certain DA offices centered on prosecutors sending out plea offers without supervisor approval. Similar to releasing a defendant against policy, in certain circumstances, if you offered a plea and the defendant received a more favorable sentence than he or she should have under the internal guidelines, you might be in for a serious reprimand (if someone found out).

These rigid guidelines made it difficult to negotiate with your colleagues on the defense bar or explain your decision to disapproving judges. The judges and defense attorneys were aware of your status as a vessel carrying out the demands of the office, but that never stopped them from expressing their discontent with your decision on the record—perhaps hoping you would change your mind or maybe simply to release their frustration with the office's position on you.

Initially, I played things safe. Inexperience only enhanced my fears of making a mistake, so I erred on the side of caution, which usually meant rarely, if ever, cutting defendants a break. There were times I felt the circumstances did not warrant detention or punishment, despite the internal recommendation, still I refrained from gambling and usually left the decision to the judge. However, I recall one day I was going through several arraignments—hearings where the defendants are made aware of the charges against them and a judge determines whether or not they should be released—and I came across a man who was charged with theft. He was facing detention due to his long criminal record, which consisted of similar theft related misdemeanors. His defense attorney made a heartfelt plea to the court for his client's release on the condition that his client undergo mental health treatment while his client's case was pending. The man's demeanor and record clearly suggested mental health issues. The man stood next to his attorney weeping loudly and wreaking of urine. I looked at the case file and saw my office's request for detention circled on the front of the case file. In my mind, I knew this man really needed treatment and not more time in a cell. When the judge asked my position, I asked her to release the defendant. She looked at me quizzically, undoubtedly confused about the difference between this defendant and the twenty others before him who I had sent to the holding cell. Despite her valid quizzical looks, she released the defendant upon my request. The man stopped crying and thanked me as he left the courtroom.

The next day I was scheduled to be in the intake room processing cases for people who were arrested the night before. I skimmed the list of names of defendants from the previous night's lockups and suddenly my heart dropped. I recognized the name of the same defendant who I had released the day prior. There were several columns on the screen that provided information about the nature of the case, so I scrolled through them quickly to determine the charges. I breathed a sigh of relief when I saw the charge was only for misdemeanor unlawful entry. Apparently, shortly after the court released the defendant, he entered, and refused to leave, a convenience store that previously barred him. For a moment, I reclined back in my chair and thought to myself, "what if he would have killed someone?" My career would have been over. This was my reward for giving him a second chance? Never again.

My paranoia surged even higher when two weeks later another one of my cases took an unexpected turn. We charged one of my misdemeanor defendants with violating the Bail Reform Act; put simply, he failed to show up for a court date. His underlying charge was voyeurism for walking into a women's restroom and using his camera phone to videotape women sitting on the toilet. During the pendency of that case, he picked up another charge for missing court. He eventually took a plea in the voyeurism case leaving pending the charge for skipping court. Bail Reform Act cases were relatively simple to prove: you needed the court docket to show that the person missed court and if the accused wasn't in the hospital or incapacitated in some way on the missed court date, you had your conviction. One wrinkle did exist. You needed at least one officer who could testify that the person in the courtroom was the same person involved in the underlying case for which he or she missed court. Unfortunately, I failed to notify the officer about the court date and the judge dismissed the case on a technicality. The defendant walked free. Frankly, I didn't think twice about it because dozens of cases were dismissed daily and went unnoticed. Two days later my supervisor called me into her office late in the afternoon.

"Pull up a seat," she said as she ended her phone conversation. "Do you recall a defendant named Thomas Jones?"

"Yeah, I think so," I said, vaguely remembering.

"What happened with that case, why was it dismissed?" she responded.

"The case was dismissed because we didn't have a witness present," I explained.

"Oh, well. It looks like the guy left jail and went out and raped a nun. The press was just on the phone asking for a statement."

My body went numb. My supervisor could sense my dismay and assured me that everything would be okay. After all, there was no guarantee that a conviction would have sent him to jail. The judge could have easily released him on the misdemeanor charge and clearly there was no way to know he would go out and rape a nun. None of these logical appeals helped assuage my feelings of guilt. For a while, I saw myself becoming more and more rigid in my decision making. The fear of releasing the wrong person again appeared each time I thought about cutting one of my defendant's a break.

Each day I went to court with this hollow feeling of helplessness. Defense attorneys would often express their frustration with the rigidity of my decisions. I responded by transferring the blame to office policy and explained that despite my agreement with the defense attorney's reasoning my hands were tied. My preconceived notions of prosecutorial discretion were slowly being replaced by the real constraints of the job.

However, as I progressed through the office, I began to observe the way some of the more experienced prosecutors navigated these restrictions. I noticed at hearings some of my colleagues would subtly suggest to the court an outcome without requesting it on the record. Although they adhered to their requirement to request detention, they wouldn't follow up with any arguments supporting their position or countering the defendant's, which signaled to the judge a lack of desire to have the defendant held. I knew it wasn't a lack of preparation or supportive arguments that drove these prosecutors to act in this way. To the contrary, I learned, that these positions were frequently negotiated between the prosecutor and the defense attorney prior to the hearing. Although the judge had the final say, most judges could sense when the attorneys were in sync with a position and rarely deviated from this unstated bilateral request. I also discovered that prosecutors used the grand jury to remove themselves from the decision of dismissing a case or reducing charges. When presenting dozens of cases before different grand juries, you develop a sense for which grand juries are more liberal and which are more conservative. Nothing required a prosecutor to use a particular grand jury over another, and the presentation of a case to one grand jury over another could mean the difference in felony or misdemeanor charges or no charges at all on the same evidence. I also realized that supervisors more readily approved plea agreements that included the victim's consent. In cases where I wanted to drop charges or reduce punishment, I would probe the victim's interests in the case and look for ways to satisfy their needs while also avoiding the most punitive result.

I was finally starting to understand how to navigate through the bureaucracy without placing my career at risk or persisting with a draconian approach. Sometimes the most I could do for a defendant was remain silent during a hearing and let the judge decide her fate. Other times, I could go as far as dropping charges altogether if I was savvy enough in my approach. Justice, for me, was much more than convicting a guilty person or setting an innocent one free. It was managing the balancing act of advocating for victims and protecting the community while breaking the cycle of mass incarceration and recidivism. I had the rare opportunity to use my judgment to create my own sense of fairness in the world, one case at a time. I knew I would never receive an award for my work; the most I ever remembered was an approving head nod and thank you from the defense. My name would never show up on anyone's Top 100 Lawyers list for dismissing cases or offering favorable pleas. Many of my friends continue to half-jokingly call me Uncle Tom, Fed, or "the man". I knew that some of them viewed me, at minimum, as a participant in the administration of an unfair justice system. I understood their views, but I knew very few of them understood what it took to carry out justice fairly. The truly effective prosecutors knew that ensuring justice meant thinking beyond the myopic perspectives of outsiders and instead taking into consideration a bevy of implications that arise from their actions. The experience forever changed my views about criminal justice.

5

WHAT IS RESTORATIVE JUSTICE?

It was June 2011 and winter where I was sitting, despite consistent seventy-degree weather throughout the day. I was one of more than a dozen other U.S. and South African law students sitting in an auditorium at the University of Western Cape's study abroad program. U.S. professors taught most of the classes, except for one class, Comparative Constitutional Law. Albie Sachs—a former South African Constitutional Supreme Court Judge—taught that class. Sachs stood a 76-year-old white man with salt and pepper hair sprawled over a receding hairline. Admittedly, he wasn't exactly what I envisioned a South African Apartheid freedom fighter would look like. Were it not for the lost vision in his right eye as well as his missing right arm from an attempted car bomb assassination, I might have doubted his many stories describing his friendships with Desmond Tutu and Nelson Mandela.

Of the classes I took, Albie Sachs' proved to be the most interesting. He conducted much of the class in a lecture format guided by assigned readings of his book, *The Strange Alchemy of Life and*

Law. Most of the class felt much like watching an Apartheid special on the *History* channel with Sachs going on for hours telling us stories about the history of South Africa. In between those stories, we would discuss opinions that he wrote during his time on the Constitutional Supreme Court. He walked us through his thought process for each selected opinion. He also had his hand in drafting the bill of rights to South Africa's New Constitution offering us a rare opportunity to gain insight into the development of a democratic society in the twenty-first century.

Of the many lessons I learned from his class, the concept of restorative justice stuck with me the most. Unlike many western justice systems, which are largely punitive in nature, South Africa rests its constitutional underpinnings on the concepts of repairing and restoring the community to its rightful order. Many South Africans believed in the concept of Ubuntu, which has many different interpretations but generally means that all human life is connected and thus people should treat each other accordingly. Many of the opinions that Sachs included in his book reflected how the concepts of Ubuntu were interwoven in South African jurisprudence. I recall reading one defamation case where, instead of requiring the defendant to pay a monetary award, the court obligated the defendant to issue a public apology to the plaintiff. In South Africa, the public shame associated with apologizing in public served punishment enough; from the court's viewpoint, there was no reason to issue a monetary judgment as would have certainly been the case in most U.S. courtrooms, where a monetary award is often the sole purpose of litigation.

Nothing embodied the concept of restorative justice more than South Africa's controversial Truth and Reconciliation Commission. As its title suggests, South Africa created the Commission to uncover the truth about the atrocities committed during Apartheid and in doing so offer a sense of closure to its victims. To accomplish this goal, the Commission offered amnesty to those who had committed heinous crimes during Apartheid. In fact, Sachs himself came face-to-face with his would-be assassin, who sought amnesty for his war crimes, including an attempt on Sachs' life.

The more I read, the more I admired the South African perspective on justice. It was the direct opposite of the U.S.'s punitive, lock-everyone-up approach that inevitably led to overcrowded prisons and high recidivism. Still, at times I wondered if the philosophies that formed the basis of the South African system were quixotic and out of touch with the realities of human nature. I knew that mass incarceration was not a sustainable or effective approach to reducing or preventing crime, but I wondered how South Africa's system prevented offenders with no intentions of changing their behavior from abusing the system. I doubted my ability to accept amnesty for those who had committed crimes against me or my loved ones. I struggled to forgive my own defendants who had committed crimes against people I didn't even know. Besides, even the most law-abiding citizen might find it tempting to violate the law if the only potential consequence was public humiliation. I learned that in some cases involving crimes as serious as rape or murder, South African courts, in considering the victim's (or the victim's survivors) wishes, would significantly reduce the penalty in return for the defendant's payment of a substantial sum to the victim or their family. Three years later, I would find myself again questioning whether restorative justice was simply a philosophy best reserved for academic discussions or one suited for the practical use in the western criminal justice system.

More of the Same

A faint knock on the door awoke Donnie from his evening slumber. Not expecting company, he arose groggy and confused as to the source of the knock. He gathered what strength his sixty-five-year-old embattled body could muster and made his way to the front door. After about three minutes of getting himself together, Donnie approached the peephole and stared through to the other side.

What he saw on the other side caused him to crack a devious smile as he slowly pulled open his apartment door and let the person on the other side inside his home.

Directly upstairs from Donnie's two-bedroom apartment resided Gloria. Gloria and Donnie were no strangers to each other. Throughout their tenure at the Washington Heights apartment building in Northeast D.C., the two were entangled in a number of domestic disputes that led to police responding to their complex. Many of the conflicts involved Gloria calling the cops to report Donnie's alleged physical abuse of his girlfriend of fifteen years, Laronda Hall. Donnie naturally despised Gloria's interloping in his personal affairs and relished in any opportunities to make Gloria's life as miserable as possible. It should have come as no surprise that when Donnie received word from a source that Gloria was allegedly running a credit card scam inside her apartment he reported the incident to the police and had Gloria arrested. From that point on, the two became bitter enemies.

Gloria sat relaxed in her reclining chair watching television when she heard a loud thud, and a faint scream coming from underneath her floor. She initially ignored the sounds, but as the screams and rummaging persisted it didn't take long for her to realize what was happening. She lowered the volume on her T.V. and grabbed her cell phone.

"Hello, this is 911, what is your emergency?" said the operator.

"Yes, I need the police to come to Washington Heights, Apartment 11. This fool downstairs is beating on his girlfriend again," said Gloria.

That same night, across town, Jeremy arrived at Naresha's apartment to pick her up around 10:30 p.m. in his white 2008 Pontiac Grand Prix. When he pulled into the parking lot, he unfolded his sun visor and flipped open the mirror to evaluate his neatly kept locks in search of stray hairs or any other potential imperfections. Satisfied with his appearance, he opened the car door, stepped his 6'2, slender frame out of the driver's seat, and headed towards

Naresha's door. Inside, standing in the bathroom mirror finishing up her makeup stood Naresha. She stood about 5'5 with caramel skin and a petite frame. Naresha and Jeremy had been friends since high school and reunited when they bumped into each other at a mutual friend's house party in Southeast D.C. The night of the party the two were engaged in an hourlong conversation prompting Jeremy to ask Naresha out on a date the following week. While Jeremy knocked on the door, Naresha's phone simultaneously rang. She answered the phone before opening the door for Jeremy.

"Hello?"

"Naresha?!" said a panicked voice on the other end.

"Hold on one second, I have someone at my door."

She opened the door for Jeremy and the two smiled at each other briefly before embracing. Naresha went back to the phone call and pointed Jeremy to the couch where he sat patiently staring at his own phone.

"Hey, who's this?" responded Naresha.

"It's Gloria. Your mom is over here again and Donnie is beating on her."

Wet Behind the Ears

After about three months on the job, I had only taken one case to trial and I was anxious to increase my trial numbers. One of my colleagues was moving to another unit within the office and our supervisor wanted her to assign the Donnie Gilmore case to me. My colleague had invested a lot of time and energy in the case; I could sense that she was emotionally invested in the trial and felt nervous about handing the case over to someone with little experience. I tried my best to assuage her fears before she delivered the case file and left my office, but I doubt I succeeded, especially given my own self-doubt. When I began to dig into the history of the people involved, I understood why my colleague wanted so badly to see Donnie convicted for this offense.

Donnie had a long criminal history that dated back twenty years. His criminal background ranged from narcotics distribution to simple assault. Admittedly, Donnie's record was common amongst my defendants, especially given his age. However, I noticed that it included several arrests and charges for domestic violence, yet somehow, none of them had resulted in convictions. As I began to dig a little deeper, I found what I suspected my investigation would reveal: Donnie's prior domestic cases all involved the same victim, Laronda Hall. I searched the docket for clues and found that the court dismissed these cases at trial, which, in domestic violence cases, typically meant the victim failed to show up in court. This pattern usually meant the victim was trapped in the cycle of violence. Unfortunately, my colleague had lost all contact with Laronda and so I knew a meeting with Naresha would be my only hope of tracking her down.

The night before trial I had yet to encounter Laronda, Naresha, Gloria, or Jeremy, all of whom were key witnesses in my case. Despite dozens of calls and voice messages, no one had answered or returned my calls. It was 7:30 p.m. and I was just about to turn off the lights to my office and walk out of the door for the night when suddenly my phone rang.

"Hello?"

"Hello, can I speak to attorney Jackson please?" said an unknown voice. "This is he, how can I help you?"

"An officer came to my house and served me with a subpoena to come to court tomorrow. I have to go to work, do I really have to come to court?" she said.

"Ma'am, what's your name?" I asked.

"This is Gloria James."

I sat back down in my chair and went through my usual spiel; I explained to Gloria the importance of complying with the subpoena and the ability of the court to issue a warrant for her arrest. If she didn't show up, I had no intentions of having the police go out to her home and pick her up, but of course I didn't want to tell her that.

My luck continued when she explained that Naresha and Jeremy had received the same subpoena and were present at her home listening in on our conversation via speakerphone. I spoke to them and explained that they needed to attend court as well. My joy quickly turned to nervousness when I realized I no longer had an excuse for losing the trial. It would have been easy to explain a dismissal where my witnesses didn't show up, but now that I knew I was going to trial the pressure began to build. I hung up the phone, scooped up the case file, and put it in my backpack before I headed home for the night.

The next day, Naresha and Gloria were waiting for me in the witness room an hour before trial. Jeremy was not yet present, but I knew I could go forward without him if I needed to. Laronda was missing as well but I hadn't expected her presence since she hadn't been subpoenaed. Naresha and Gloria greeted me as soon as I entered the room. Given that they had never seen my face before, I figured they must have recognized my voice after hearing me speaking to a colleague in the hallway. The two were very pleasant and deferential. Gloria was about 5'3, 150 lbs. and fifty years of age. She had brown skin and a nonchalant look about her. She was not overly excited about having to come to court but like most witnesses, she was happy to hear about the cash voucher she would receive for appearing as a witness. She also wanted very badly to see Donnie behind bars.

"Mr. Jackson is he going to do jail time?" Gloria asked. "It's time for this to stop. This has been going on for too long."

"I'm not sure what the judge will do, but first we have to focus on the trial and your testimony," I responded.

Naresha was quiet most of the time but readily responded when I asked her questions about what happened that night. Despite having to recall an experience that she undoubtedly would like to forget, she acquiesced without anger or hesitation. Naresha had the type of magnetic personality that I knew would serve her well on the stand. She came across as honest and respectful and a little less combative than Gloria.

We left the witness room and headed towards court. As we drew closer to the courtroom, I noticed a younger man with long hair standing outside wearing distressed denim jeans and a white t-shirt. Naresha sprinted ahead in front of me and Gloria and greeted the man with an affectionate embrace. As I suspected, it was Jeremy.

I could tell by the look on his face that I was happier to see him than he was to see me.

"You the prosecutor, bruh? Man, I'm about to leave. I have to go to work. I'm not trying to be involved in this. I don't want anything to do with testifying on no stand bro," he lamented.

I was used to this routine, especially with male witnesses. In fact, I previously shared his sentiments about cooperating with law enforcement. This perspective helped me convince many of them to go forward and testify despite their opposition.

"Jeremy, I understand that you don't want to testify and you'd rather be somewhere else right now, but you are under subpoena and it's not like you asked to be here. Essentially, you have no choice," I explained.

Most witnesses seemed to feel better if they could go back and tell everyone that they were under subpoena and that the judge would have thrown them in jail had they not testified.

"Look man, to be real. I don't even remember what happened," said Jeremy.

Selective amnesia was another technique a lot of witnesses used to avoid testifying, but I had heard this excuse before and was prepared for it.

"Let me show you some of the photos of your injuries and maybe that will jog your memory," I said.

When he realized I wasn't going to let up he followed me into the witness room and we went through his testimony.

I had all my witnesses in place and I was prepared to give my opening statement. Judge Bailey took my case—the judge in front of whom I won my first trial. Judge Bailey held a reputation as an ultra-conservative member of the bench appointed during the Bush administration. My colleagues often joked that a prosecutor could convict a dead man in his courtroom. Judge Bailey frequently issued harsh sentences for misdemeanors and held people in jail with no bond for the slightest violation of release conditions. I felt good about my chances in front of him, and now that I had three witnesses I felt even better.

I walked into the courtroom and handled the calendar of cases with one of my colleagues who had a trial of her own. The calendar could range from ten to thirty or more cases set for various types of hearings or trial. Since my trial was in front of the calendar-judge, I allowed my colleague to prepare for her trial while I handled most of the hearings. There were about twenty status hearings and a few sentencings, so the heavy calendar carried us until lunch break and the Judge ordered us to return ready for trial after lunch.

Handling the hearings settled my nervousness about trial; arguing motions and making decisions on my feet was a good warm-up for what was to come, but it was also draining. I could have used that time to memorize my opening or better prepare my witnesses. Before I knew it, it was time for lunch and I had an hour before my opening statement. Gloria, Naresha, and Jeremy were all out in the hallway disappointed that the trial hadn't started earlier. I sent them to lunch with encouraging words about getting them out of court as soon as possible but I knew they would probably be there all day and maybe even the next day.

It seemed as if lunch never even happened and before I knew it Judge Bailey called us to the bench to start trial. My opponent held a reputation for his courtroom antics. He too suffered from selective amnesia, often conveniently forgetting whether or not the prosecutor had provided him with certain evidence. If you failed to keep track of your discovery, he would claim missing evidence and seek a continuance. This decreased the likelihood of your witnesses showing up again for trial and increased his chances of the court dismissing the case. Equally annoying were his trial tactics.

He extended cross-examinations for hours asking the same questions over and over despite repeated objections. Judge Bailey would usually allow these shenanigans to avoid successful appeals based on technical issues. He preferred to rule on a case based solely on witness testimony, which made for an airtight verdict. Bailey acted as judge and jury, so the appellate court could not overturn rulings regarding credibility of witnesses. Unsurprisingly, nearly all of Judge Bailey's rulings came down to credibility. Bailey would suppress your evidence, deny your motions, and still convict based solely on the testimony of the parties. It was great if you were a prosecutor but terrifying if you were a defendant—your conviction could hinge on the word of one person.

The trial began, and I put my strongest witness on the stand first to tell the story about what happened that night.

Me: Naresha, could you tell the court what it is you do for a living?

Naresha: Right now, I am unemployed. I just recently finished high school and was supposed to go to college, but I found out that I have cervical cancer and had to undergo surgery. I couldn't afford school after the medial bills started coming in.

Me: Naresha, do you know a person by the name of Donnie Gilmore?

Naresha: Yes, he is my mom's ex-boyfriend.

Me: And is he in the courtroom today?

Naresha: Yes, he is the man sitting at that table with dark skin wearing the orange jumpsuit and grey beard.

Me: Let the record reflect an in-court identification of the defendant your honor.

Judge Bailey: Noted.

Me: Could you described your relationship with Mr. Gilmore?

Naresha: I don't care for Donnie. He has been abusing my mother for years.

Defense: Objection your honor, this is hearsay and not relevant and highly prejudicial.

Me: Your honor, this is relevant to Naresha's state of mind when she visited the defendant's apartment. This statement is not being offered for its truth.

Judge Bailey: Overruled, you may proceed.

Naresha: Donnie knows that my mother is addicted to drugs and he provides the drugs for her. I've witnessed him assault my mother and he has assaulted me before as well. My mom is vulnerable because of her addiction and he uses her.

At this point, Naresha began to cry on the stand. I looked over towards Donnie and saw him grinning from the defense table. I could tell he enjoyed the sense of control he got from seeing Naresha in pain. Judge Bailey offered Naresha some tissue for her wet eyes which caused a brief pause in the proceedings. I felt sorry for Naresha and her situation. She was a good person who had been dealt a tough hand in life having an addict for a mother and developing cancer at such a young age. Donnie only made it worse by victimizing her mother who was now living on the streets with no place to go.

Me: Naresha, could you explain to the court what happened after you received that phone call from Gloria?

Naresha: I told Jeremy what had happened. He could tell by my face something was wrong and when I told him, he asked me what I was going to do. I asked him if he would take me to my mom and he said yes. We were only about fifteen minutes away so we got there kinda fast.

Me: What happened when you got there?

Naresha: When I got to Donnie's door, I started banging on it and yelling for him to let my mother out of there.

Me: Where was Jeremy at this point?

Naresha: Jeremy was still in the car, which was around the corner parked in the parking lot. I told him that I would be right back once I got my mom, so he didn't get out. A few minutes after I started beating on the door, I saw Gloria come from her upstairs apartment down to where I was at. Then soon after that the door opened.

Me: What happened next?

Naresha: Donnie came to the door asking why I was banging on his door. I started yelling at him to let my mom out of his apartment and we started cursing at each other while he was standing near the door. Eventually, I saw my mom appear from the back and I could see that she had a bruise on her right eye and cuts on her face. When I saw her, I snapped. I grabbed her arm and yanked her out of the apartment into the grassy area in front of the house.

Me: Then what happened?

Naresha: I guess Jeremy must have heard all the noise and he started walking towards us trying to separate everybody. That's when Donnie pulled out his wooden cane and start swinging it at everyone. I got hit over the head with the cane. When I grabbed my head because of the pain I could see Gloria grabbing her head too. That's when I noticed Jeremy's nose was bleeding and Donnie was running away.

Me: What did Donnie do after he hit everyone with the cane?

Naresha: I saw him running away. I was helping Jeremy, so I didn't see where he went but he was long gone by the time the police came.

Me: Did you ever threaten Donnie that night?

Naresha: No.

Me: Did you hear or observe Jeremey or Gloria threaten Donnie that night?

Naresha: No.

Me: Did you observe Jeremy or Gloria strike Donnie?

Naresha: No, no one touched him.

This was all I needed for a conviction. Naresha was clearly telling the truth and I could tell by the judge's facial expressions that he had already made up his mind. But, for Donnie's defense attorney, the battle had just begun. He began by cross-examining Naresha, trying his best to establish her disdain for Donnie. The defense's theory was that Gloria and Naresha conspired to retaliate against Donnie for past offenses.

Defense: When you heard what Gloria had told you over the phone, you wanted revenge didn't you?

Naresha: I just wanted to make sure my mom was okay.

Defense: You and Jeremy were going down there to set my client straight weren't you? At all costs!

Naresha: No, I told you why we were going there.

The defense's aggressive strategy might have worked if Naresha was lying, but she wasn't. She answered questions in the indignant way you'd expect someone who is being challenged about telling the truth to respond. Her calmness only vexed the defense attorney even more causing him to ask repetitive questions which started to frustrate the judge. Eventually, he gave up and Naresha was able to step down from the witness stand.

Next up to the stand came Jeremy. His diffident demeanor proved as equally effective as Naresha's. He sat back in his seat expressing his discontent about having to testify, but the judge reprimanded him and asked that he sit forward. Jeremy leaned forward begrudgingly tightening up his posture as I began my direct examination. During my questioning, Jeremy came across as annoyed and provided terse responses, yet his testimony matched Naresha's and that's all that really mattered. He clearly had become a casualty of war in this incident. He had no idea what he was getting himself into when Naresha asked him to accompany her to Donnie's apartment. Frankly, he didn't want to go, but he saw the anger and fear in Naresha's eyes and felt obligated to do something. The defense fared no better in rattling him. Jeremy, however, found it more difficult than Naresha to hide his frustration with the redundancy of the questioning.

Defense: You went over to my client's home to teach him a lesson, didn't you?

Jeremy: What are talking about man? I told you the only reason I went over there was because Resha asked me to. I've told you that like five times now.

Defense: Objection your honor.

Judge: I'll ask the witness to just answer the question, please. Counsel, I will note that you've asked this question several times already. Could you please move on?

I didn't even bother objecting to his repetitive questioning. Had this been in front of the jury, I might have done so, but his constant badgering of the witness annoyed the judge, so I just let him hang himself. Once the defense finished, I asked a few follow-up questions to solidify Jeremy's testimony.

Me: Jeremy, before you were struck with the cane, had you threatened the defendant?

Had you struck him or attempted to strike him?

Jeremey: No.

Me: No further questions your honor.

Gloria was my last witness. I knew she was not my strongest, so I wanted her to testify in the middle to begin and finish strong. However, Jeremy had already missed a day of work and he begged me to get his testimony over with as soon as I could. I knew his compliance with the subpoena was hanging on by a thread and I realized how important the money was to him, so I agreed. On the third day of trial, Gloria took the stand. I knew the defense would call into question her bias towards Donnie, so I brought out those facts early in her testimony. She admitted that she didn't like Donnie and that he accused her of running a credit card scam but she had never been convicted of anything related to those allegations.

Once we raised these issues, I moved on to the incident. Gloria explained how she heard loud noises coming from Donnie's apartment that night and decided to investigate. She witnessed Donnie assault Laronda numerous times and assumed this was just another occasion. She went down to the front of Donnie's apartment and attempted to investigate by peering through the blindless window. From the window, she saw Donnie striking Laronda with his fists and dragging her across the floor. She called the police, but by the time they arrived the noise had stopped, and Donnie refused to answer the door. Since the police didn't have a warrant, and they hadn't witnessed the crime themselves they couldn't go into Donnie's home and substantiate the claim, so they left. That's when Gloria called Naresha. Throughout her testimony, I could feel Donnie's laser stare burning a hole through Gloria's face as she described what happened.

When I completed my direct examination, the defense approached and began cross-examination. As predicted, Gloria became defensive on the stand. The defense attorney appeared invigorated at his first opportunity to poke holes in our case. His theory was that Gloria had orchestrated this entire incident to get back at Donnie for exposing her alleged credit card scheme. He quizzed her on why the police would come and leave if an actual crime had been committed. To make matters worse, we had no record of the 911 call or a report memorializing Gloria's call. The defense drilled her on both gaps in evidence. Although missing 911 calls were common and police rarely made reports for non-arrests; nevertheless, the missing evidence served as a significant blow to our case given that we couldn't find anything in the system that corroborated Gloria's police report. I hoped Gloria could survive cross-examination without any significant mishaps. Luckily, the defense's sixty-minute cross did little damage to my case and I rested with Gloria serving as my final witness.

After I rested my case, the defense put Donnie on the stand. The move came as no surprise. Testifying represented Donnie's only shot at an acquittal. Frankly, Donnie held a viable self-defense claim. He was a 65-year-old man who owned a cane—though my witnesses testified they never saw him use it to walk. From Donnie's perspective, three angry people confronted him at his home to protect a supposed victim who hadn't even shown up to court. Maybe my case wasn't as strong as I initially thought.

Defense: Donnie, could you tell us what happened the night you were assaulted?

Donnie: I was in my apartment with Laronda. She came over asking me for some crack and I told her to leave, but she wouldn't leave.

Defense: Did you ever hit her that night?

Donnie: No, I just told her to leave my house but she didn't leave.

Defense: How did she get the bruises on her face?

Donnie: I don't know, those bruises were old.

Defense: What happened next?

Donnie: I left my house because I didn't want to be around her. When I left my house and started walking around the corner, I saw Gloria standing outside looking at me. I kept walking but then a white car pulled up.

Defense: What did the white car do?

Donnie: It pulled up right next to me and two people jumped out. It was Naresha and the dude with dreads who testified earlier. Naresha had a knife in her hand and the dude with the dreads just started running towards me.

Defense: What did you do?

Donnie: I tried to run but I couldn't get far because I walk with a cane. They closed in on me, so I picked up my cane to fight back. The boy with the dreads grabbed my cane and Naresha was trying to stab me with the knife. I was fighting them both back with both hands.

Defense: Do you remember the guy with dreads getting his nose broken?

Donnie: Yes, when he was pulling for the stick, he pulled so hard that I let it go and he got hit in the nose with the stick. That's when I fell to the ground and they started stomping me! They crushed my leg. My leg looked like spaghetti. Then I ran to the window screaming for help but no one was coming and I saw Gloria standing there laughing.

Defense: How did you get away?

Donnie: I ran to one of my friend's house close by and he let me in.

At this point, it took everything in me not to burst out laughing in the courtroom. I tried my best to maintain my composure by placing my open right hand on my chin while staring at Donnie as if I was in deep reflection about his testimony. The only thing I was reflecting on was how ridiculous his story sounded. The judge stared incredulously at his notepad scribbling notes and cutting the occasional side-eye in the direction of Donnie's animated testimony. His defense attorney's willingness to allow his client to present such a patently false story to the court surprised me. When Donnie finally finished, I sat for a few seconds and pushed aside the notes that I had prepared the night before. I could wing this one.

Me: Mr. Gilmore, so you were fighting with Mr. Brooks?

Donnie: Who?

Me: The person with dreads that you mentioned.

Donnie: Yes.

Me: You were fighting with him and you two were struggling over your cane?

Donnie: That's right, he attacked me!

Me: And Naresha had a knife, correct?

Donnie: That's what I said.

Me: So, how were you struggling with Mr. Brooks with your cane and fighting off Naresha who you said had a knife in her hand?

Donnie: I had one hand on the cane and one hand on her wrist.

Me: So, you were able to hold both Naresha and Mr. Brooks back at the same time?

Donnie: That's right.

Me: And you fell to the ground and they started stomping you right?

Donnie: Yes!

Me: You said your leg was crushed by the stomping?

Donnie: That's right, they broke my leg.

Me: Then how were you able to run to the window and ask for help and get away to your friend's apartment?

Donnie: You'd be surprised at what you can do when you're fighting for your life!

I could have gone on for much longer, but I knew it wasn't worth it. There was something pitiful about standing there listening to Donnie lie on the stand. I felt sorry for him. I sat down and knew that the rest of the trial was a formality. We gave our closing statements and the despite the late hour, the judge told us that he would have a verdict within an hour, which meant he had already made up his mind. When we returned, to no one's surprise Judge Bailey returned a verdict of guilty on all counts except for assault on Laronda, who hadn't shown up for trial. Bailey did not credit Gloria's testimony that she had observed, through the window, Donnie strike Laronda, so, at sentencing, Donnie would be facing three counts of assault as opposed to four, which didn't make much of a difference.

Donnie's defense attorney pled with me not to send his client to jail. After the judge read the verdict, for the first time, I saw a look of fear and shame on Donnie's face. When Judge Bailey asked whether Donnie should be held in prison pending sentencing, I looked over to Donnie as he stared back at me with a look of pity. I caved and decided to let him free pending sentencing. The judge was shocked, and I could tell he was close to overriding my suggestion and holding Donnie anyway. I knew it was risky, but I figured if Albie Sachs could forgive the man who attempted to murder him, surely, I could forgive Donnie for his crimes.

A week before sentencing, I received a call from Naresha. She thanked me for all my hard work on the case. I asked if she wanted to be present for sentencing, she said that she couldn't make it because she needed to go through chemotherapy again. She wanted me to know that she hadn't found her mother yet, but that she heard Donnie was in the neighborhood still harassing her mother and Gloria. It upset her that the judge had let him out of court and not put him in jail. I listened to her rant, too ashamed to tell her that I had recommended Donnie's release. I thanked her for the information and agreed to convey her message to the court at sentencing. Ironically, right when she called, I was preparing my sentencing recommendation for Donnie. Initially, I recommended probation but Naresha's news changed my mind. Donnie had ruined not only Laronda's life but her daughter's as well. I thought about the intimidating looks he flashed Naresha while she testified. I reflected on how brazenly and nonchalantly he perjured himself in court. I became angered when I realized that his flashes of remorse were nothing more than an attempt to avoid punishment. To add insult to injury, I had given him another chance at redemption and he had used that opportunity to continue his abuse of Naresha's vulnerable and broken mother. Donnie was the type of defendant that I feared restorative justice would enable. A person intent on exploiting any weakness he could find in the system with no intentions of ever changing. I knew at that point that even if prison was not the answer for Donnie, freedom wasn't either. At sentencing, Donnie and his attorney had no idea that I would seek the maximum sentence, 180 days of prison on each count; especially given my leniency after the verdict, and their ignorance to my haven spoken to Naresha. Judges rarely sentenced a defendant to over a year in prison for misdemeanors, so I doubted the court would grant my request, but I felt it was fair given Donnie's history and continued violations. Unfortunately, I couldn't attend the hearing, because I had another trial on the same day, so one of my colleagues handled it. When I got back from my trial, I stopped by my colleagues' office.

Me: Hey, what happened with that sentencing for Donnie Gilmore?

Colleague: Oh, you mean the old guy with the cane?

Me: Yeah (I laughed), how did you remember? I know you guys had thirty cases on calendar.

Colleague: The judge slammed him, that's why! What the hell did he do? Yeah, the guy got a year and a half of straight jail time.

Me: Damn.

I called to give Naresha the news, but she didn't pick up, so I reached out to Gloria. She was happy to hear the news; I could tell that my call had brightened her day. Not too long after I hung up the phone, Donnie's lawyer called me pissed about my request. He sought a rehearing which the judge rejected. I sat in my office after the call thinking about what I had learned in South Africa and whether my views towards the criminal justice system had changed. They hadn't. I still believed in restorative justice, but I also believed that it only worked for those who were willing to accept responsibility for their actions and embrace change. In fact, I realized that this was the message Albie Sachs wanted us to understand all along. Restorative justice didn't mean a free pass, but rather a chance for each man or woman, as Brian Stevenson once stated, "to prove that he [or she] is better than the worst thing that he [or she] has done" in life. Justice meant that Donnie would get a year and a half to reflect on that missed opportunity.

WAR

"War does not determine who is right – only who is left."

—BERTRAND RUSSELL

The legal system in the United States is described as adversarial, but any litigator will tell you that this description is a gross understatement. Whether civil or criminal, litigation in the U.S. is all-out war. Unlike the inquisitorial system (used in many European countries) where judges are at the center of the investigative process, the adversarial system in the U.S. relies largely on the two parties (primarily the two lawyers) pitted against one another to ferret out the truth. Unfortunately, the pursuit of truth is not always at the forefront of the lawyers' minds, winning is. As a result, the system becomes a reflection of the imbalances created by capitalism as opposed to an institution that ensures a fair outcome for both sides.

Given the stakes, you would think the architects of the criminal justice system would seek to eliminate these inequities. Admittedly, there are several amendments to the U.S. Constitution aimed at protecting the criminally accused that do not apply in the civil context. The basic principle of these amendments is that when a person's liberty is at stake, the burden should be on the state to establish that a citizen's rights have not been violated or that the accused is guilty of the offense as charged. In practice, these protections are only affective when you have a quality defense lawyer, which usually isn't a public defender and costs more than most defendants can afford. In white-collar criminal cases, it is not uncommon for the defendant to have just as many, if not more, resources as the state. In my time working for a few of the top law firms in the country, I saw white-collar criminal defendants enlist dozens of attorneys who worked around the clock to fight charges lodged against them by government agencies. Many times, these agencies' lawyers are overworked and underpaid and do not have the manpower to lock horns with major law firms. Consequently, the government will frequently settle for a monetary payment by the corporation in return for a deferred prosecution agreement. Although government agencies have recently placed a priority on prosecuting corporate officers who commit white collar crimes, convictions—and certainly jail time—for these wealthy defendants are the exception and not the rule. The same cannot be said for your garden variety robbery or murder suspect, where the accused is unlikely to have the resources of a large company to employ a law firm to protect his or her rights. Instead, an overworked and underpaid public defender will have to suffice. In non-white collar criminal cases, the state holds most of the resources and has the power to determine the fate of the accused, who is often poor and unfamiliar with the criminal justice system.

As a prosecutor investigating local crimes, you are the general of the army initiating the war against the defendant. In most instances, you have more weapons, more troops, and you hold the element of surprise. You have the power to call an end to the war at any time or decide to decimate the enemy. In an ideal criminal justice system, the prosecutor would only concern herself with seeking the truth and determining the just result given the circumstances. Unfortunately, the adversarial system does not promote this view-point. The legal profession breeds fighters. From the day you sit for the LSAT up until the day you take the bar, you are compet-ing against your peers for scholarships, to graduate at the top of the class, to earn a spot on law journal or moot court, to secure a position at a top law firm or clerkship, and the list goes on. From your first year as a law student up until you enter the field of law you are told to advocate for your client at all costs, short of placing your license in jeopardy. You are told that clients do not want to hear excuses, they want results. You are trained to defend the undefendable and advocate without regard to emotions. Combine this culture of competitiveness with a population of A-type personality, egocentric and self-righteous people and you have the "adversarial system" in America.

Prosecutors are not immune from this aggressive mind-set. In fact, the promotional structure in most district attorneys' offices across the country encourage this behavior. Not once in my entire time as a prosecutor did I see anyone receive an award for losing a tough case or dropping charges. Prosecutors receive little to no recognition for dismissing cases or offering equitable pleas. Despite the "winning isn't everything" rhetoric we heard repeatedly at meetings, everyone knew success meant winning trials and getting convictions. Taking losing cases or "dogs" (as our office often called them) to trial and winning was viewed as a major accomplishment. Usually "dog" cases came with significant issues that reduced the likelihood of success, e.g. witness credibility issues, weak evidence, or a strong defense. I often wondered why we took these cases to trial anyway; I always felt uncomfortable advocating for conviction without complete confidence that I could prove the case beyond a reasonable doubt.

The competitive nature of the system also created a cloud of distrust and scorn that permeated the relationships among its major players. As a prosecutor, you must be ever vigilant for defense attorneys who are out to win at all costs without regard to ethical rules. They will smile in your face before a hearing and then lie to the judge about evidence you supposedly withheld or witnesses you wouldn't allow them to access. Whatever they must do to make you look bad in front of the judge, they have no qualms about doing it and pretending as if nothing ever happened once the hearing was over. Some prosecutors hold an "us against them" view of the defense bar, clinging to vendettas against specific defense attorneys for various past offenses and cherishing opportunities to return the favor. Unfortunately, the defendant ultimately suffers and has nothing to do with the opposing attorneys' feud. The judge also plays a role in the ongoing battles. Most of the judges take their oaths to be impartial decision makers very seriously, and do their best to treat both sides equally, despite their personal viewpoints. Other judges appear hell-bent on engineering an outcome.

The worst part about the intersecting wars that go on every day in criminal courts around the country is that, much like real war, there are no winners, only casualties on both sides. Most times, the casualties are the most vulnerable in our society, the uninformed, poor, addicted, and disabled. The victims in the criminal cases I prosecuted rarely felt more than a fleeting sense of fulfillment about a guilty plea or verdict. Many of them simply wanted the person to stay away from them or pay for their financial losses. Frankly, most of the victims wanted nothing to do with the process and either feared retaliation after guilty verdicts or had lost faith in the system when defendants walked free.

For the defendant, the war proved equally unwinnable. Even if she walked away without a conviction, the inconvenience of court appearances, paying lawyers and the stress of fighting criminal charges remained. I saw defendants sit in jail for months and lose their employment on cases that were eventually dismissed. The accused returned home to mounting bills and no job, without as much as an apology from anyone in the courtroom. Those who are guilty and convicted of crimes rarely received the rehabilitation that they needed. Prison is one of the most counter-rehabilitative institutions on the planet and probation rarely addressed the mental health issues and drug addictions that many defendants struggle with. For those who were somehow rehabilitated, the stamp of convict awaited with all the collateral consequences that accompanied the title.

The more cases I prosecuted, the more I realized the fundamental flaws underpinning our criminal justice system. Every day, as a prosecutor, I battled two forces: an external battle with the judges,

lawyers and office politics alongside an internal battle with my conscious and the guilt I felt serving as an agent of a completely broken
system. There were times where the parties all came together to
ensure the best outcome possible given the circumstances, but these
occasions occurred far less than I hoped. In time, my biggest fears
began to materialize as I saw myself becoming yet another soldier
in an unwinnable war.

6

I GOT THIS!

I was sitting in my office thumbing through case files with my door open when the phone rang. I recognized the number as Patricia Tully's—Tim Jones' defense attorney, from several back and forth calls about the upcoming trial. Her client faced 10 years in prison on an armed robbery charge and we had him dead to rights. For the past month, I made dozens of attempts to contact Ms. Tully about a potential resolution to the case to no avail, but it wasn't until twenty-four hours prior to trial that Jones' attorney finally responded.

"Mr. Jackson, I think we can settle this case," she said. "My client is willing to take one count of robbery, if the government will drop the remaining charges."

Patricia and I both knew a plea to robbery was a slap on the wrist considering the number of years her client was facing if a jury found him guilty of the charges in the indictment. Defense attorneys frequently solicited low ball offers during the early investigation stages of the case, but such a proposal just hours before trial was laughable.

"Ms. Tully, we offered you armed robbery months ago, why would we drop it down to robbery just before trial?"

"My client isn't willing to take a plea that involves a minimum of 5 years in jail. He won't even consider it," she said.

"I'll talk to my supervisor."

I used this response when I had no intentions of negotiating further and I wanted to transfer the blame to a third party. I simply couldn't justify letting Ms. Tully's client off the hook on the eve of trial with a robbery plea after months of preparation. Plus, I had just won two difficult trials in a row that appeared unwinnable at the outset, and my confidence level was high. My trial partner, David, was less confident.

"I think we should take a hard look at this offer. This case may not be as rock solid as you think," David stated as we discussed the case in my office.

"Man, we've put in all this work. Tully has had months to take a plea and now her client finally comes to his senses? Whatever, I'm willing to talk to Tiffany about the plea offer if you want, but we can win this thing."

"A conviction is better than a not guilty. If he walks, we've got nothing," David explained.

I disagreed with David, but I respected his opinion. He was a seasoned trial attorney who had tried homicides in another juris-diction. He had taken dozens of cases to trial before joining the office, and I often sought his advice when I needed help preparing for trial. This was our second trial together, so out of respect for our friendship, I agreed to have a sit down with our supervisor and discuss the last-minute plea, even though I hated the idea of offering a plea. We walked into our supervisor's office and sat down on her couch to explain our situation. Apparently, Jones was also a target witness in one of Tiffany's cases so, given the conflict of interest, she recused herself and directed us to the chief of our homicide division for guidance.

We took the elevator to the homicide division and within min-utes found ourselves sitting in front of the chief's desk discussing the case. This was David's case, so he took the lead on the conversation.

He explained the timeline of events and his views on the likelihood of us obtaining a conviction. He then asked the chief, Lauren, her opinion about whether we should accept the plea offer or counter with one of our own. I sat silently listening to the exchange, not wanting to interject my strong opposition to a plea. If things went wrong, I didn't want to have gone on the record opposing a plea, despite my aversion to the idea.

"Martinis, what do you think?" She asked.

I paused for a minute.

"I think we have a strong case. Our witnesses are ready and we have video footage. I'm not enthusiastic about extending a plea this late in the game. It sets a bad precedent." I responded.

What I really wanted to say but couldn't was that I wanted the additional trial experience and I felt cocky given my recent victories, but I figured those reasons wouldn't have been as persuasive.

I refrained from looking directly at David as I figured he wouldn't be stoked about my response. I noticed him in the corner of my eye as he exhaled heavily and crossed his arms undoubtedly vexed by my cockiness. He had been fighting the flu the past few days and I could tell the virus was taking its toll on him. David preferred a plea over a weeklong trial, but my ego couldn't let this opportunity to bolster my trial experience go to waste.

Lauren looked at both of us.

"I'll leave the decision to both of you. I'll authorize a plea, but you can decide whether or not you want to extend it. You know the case better than I do." She said.

We left Lauren's office and headed down the hall towards the elevator. David was quiet until I broke the silence.

"I think we can win this case man, but I'm down for whatever you want to do. If you want to offer the plea, let's do it." I told David.

In the end, we decided to offer a modified version of the plea which included some mandatory jail time. David was a reasonable person and despite his desire to resolve the case, he decided to meet me halfway. We called Patricia around 10:00 p.m. and conveyed the offer via speakerphone. She said she would get back to us the next day.

The Robbery

It was May 2015 and William was careening down the street on his skateboard, a grey cruiser that he had been riding since high school. He thrust a few forceful kicks to the ground with his right leg as he picked up speed before he placed both feet on the board and navigated through the pothole riddled D.C. streets. On his back rested a black backpack with his production equipment: A Canon EOS with three lenses, a flood light, and a camera stand. He was running late to a video shoot for an old high school classmate named Roderick Parker, aka Big Rod. William hadn't produced a rap video for a local artist in three years and was excited to return to his craft. He fell in love with cinematography at a young age; in high school he entered a competition to produce a short film using the school's primitive hardware and software. William's project was a PowerPoint presentation of urban photography. The judges praised his natural ability to capture the beauty in everyday urban life. He won first place and claimed the Canon EOS as his prize.

William shot his first video for Big Rod during his junior year of high school. Rod was a local gangster rapper whose lyrical content often referenced using firearms and selling narcotics, content that closely reflected his lifestyle. Rod's music was beginning to garner a small following in the community, but he wanted to promote his songs through YouTube to capture a larger audience and he knew William could do the job at a cheap price. At Rod's request, William shot Rod's first video, titled *Loyalty*, at night on a vacant playground with several the members of Rod's entourage. Rod paid William $100 for the video and looked forward to working with William on future projects.

Unfortunately for Rod, William decided to take a hiatus from shooting videos and focus on still photography. He shot one more video for Rod but ignored many of Rod's future Facebook messages to shoot videos. For a few years, Rod struggled to find a replacement producer but made due by paying other freelance shooters who provided similar quality videos for higher prices.

A few years later, Rod reached out to William again, but this time William agreed to shoot a video at a local community center during the day for $150. William asked his close friend, Reggie, to accompany him on the shoot and help with lighting and assist with coordinating the shoot. When William pulled up on his skateboard, Rod and about fifteen members of his entourage were already present outside of the community center. Before the shoot, William noticed a person with a blue shirt and dreadlocks in the distance call out to the group.

"Yo! When yall coming to the spot?" said the person in the blue shirt.

"We'll be over there in about 20 minutes," said one of Rod's associates.

William listened in as Rod's associate speculated about the identity of the person in the blue shirt and dreadlocks.

"I think that was Jerrell." Said Rod's associate.

"Nah, I bet that was Tim." Responded Rod.

"How do you know?" Asked Rod's associate.

"Just trust me." Rod stated confidently.

William thought nothing of the exchange and continued shooting for another fifteen minutes before Rod requested the video shoot move to a different location. William and Reggie packed up their equipment and walked about seven blocks to the new venue. The area was elevated and enclosed by a fence on three sides and offered only two entry points, one—a seven-foot drop over an iron gate and the other—fifteen feet of stairs leading to the street. After a few minutes at the new location, William grew impatient with the shoot. Oddly, Rod seemed overly critical of his work, requesting several retakes of simple shots and asking to review the footage every few seconds.

"Man, can we hurry this shit along? We've been doing nothing for the past few minutes. There's nothing wrong with this shot bro." lamented William.

"The lighting isn't right Mo, I don't like how my face looks on this one." Responded Rod.

After a few more minutes of loitering, William saw two men emerge from the stairs. One was a tall brown-skinned male with dreadlocks wearing a blue jacket and carrying a firearm and other man wore a white coat and a mask covering his face also pointing a gun in the group's direction.

As the two men approached, many of the members of Rod's crew scattered running past the two assailants without hesitation. The man in the dreads walked up to Rod and demanded his cell phone. Immediately, Rod handed over his device. Meanwhile, Reggie had taken his chances with the seven-foot drop and hopped the iron fence landing nimbly on his feet on the other side. William was trapped. The man with the mask seemed focused on him from the outset. He approached William and jerked his backpack from his back spinning him around with his free hand while pointing the gun in the other. William fell to the ground but resisted as a brief struggle ensued. The man with the dreads shifted his focus toward the scuffle and immediately pointed his gun towards William prompting William to refrain from resisting. With William's bag in tow, the two gunmen fled down the stairs on foot, leaving William, Rod, and one of Rod's associates—Don, on the enclosed grassy knoll.

When Reggie realized the coast was clear, he returned to the hill where William was walking frantically back and forth speaking with the emergency dispatcher about the Robbery.

"It was a brown skinned guy with dreads and another guy with a mask. Both of them had guns," he said.

Reggie was happy to see that his friend hadn't been shot. He also noticed William's missing camera and backpack and immediately realized the implication. Their fears turned to anger as the two set out to find the culprits but quickly gave up pursuit when they failed to determine in which direction the robbers had fled. William decided to return to the community center where many of Rod's entourage, who had not accompanied him to the second shoot, remained. Rod's crew was known to carry firearms and they had a reputation of retaliating for the slightest infraction. Yet when William returned to explain what happened to Rod many of them responded nonchalantly.

William and Reggie spoke with the police that evening and made a report about the events that unfolded that afternoon. Rod was not present during the report and he never reached out to William after the incident. In fact, the two never spoke again.

That night William laid in his bed brooding over his camera and the robbery. He started to conduct his own investigation. He pondered the identity of the person in the blue jacket with dreads at the community center and doubted it was a coincidence that he fit the description of one of the robbers. The robbers knew exactly what they were looking for; how were they so lucky to find the group in such a secluded area? Why didn't Rod or his crew seem more concerned about the robbery? A few weeks later, William took to social media and browsed Rod's Instagram page and noticed that Rod had recently posted a new video that appeared to have been shot with William's camera. One of William's lenses had a scratch which appeared in his videos and helped him identify his work. He recognized the subtle mark from years of shooting and taking photos. He also observed in the music video two handguns of the exact same make and model as the ones the suspects used during the robbery. He then went to Rod's YouTube page and began reviewing old videos. Ten seconds into playing "Loyalty" and he immediately paused the screen, the frame showed Rod embracing the two young men: William had never seen the young kid to Rob's left before; however, to Rod's right stood the man who had robbed William a few weeks ago.

William called the detective he met on the day of the robbery. The detective brought William in the next day to participate in a photo array procedure. The nine-person photo array included eight decoy suspects—who also had shoulder length locks and brown complexion—and the target. With confidence, William selected Tim Jones as the person who had robbed him. The same Tim Jones from the music video.

Our investigation revealed evidence that supported William's conspiracy theory. When we subpoenaed Rod's phone records, Rod's call logs revealed that, immediately after the robbery, he dialed several previously dialed numbers. This suggested that Tim returned the phone to Rod right after the robbery. Surveillance video showed a person with Tim's same height, hairstyle and jacket running up the stairs with his hand in his right pocket suggestive of gripping a firearm. The film depicted the two suspects walking directly to the group despite the secluded nature of their where-abouts. Rod came to our office and to no one's surprise denied Tim's involvement in the robbery. A month later, the police arrested Rod for attempted murder; he later pled guilty and began serving a lengthy sentence in federal prison. The unrelated case summary stated that Rod had shot and robbed the victim. I doubted that Tim's defense attorney would put a convicted felon on the stand despite Tim's cryptic jail calls begging his family members to get Rod to testify on his behalf. If he did, even better, I would crucify Rod on the stand. When David and I met with William and Reggie, we knew they would come across as great witnesses. Both were college students with no criminal records. Reggie was active in his community. In his free time, he helped the homeless find housing. William worked part time as an Uber Eats delivery person. The two young men were humble and straight forward about what happened. There were minor inconsistencies in their stories: Reggie recalled the person with dreads carrying a revolver, but William believed it was a semi-automatic. Other issues existed as well:

Reggie was never presented with a photo array and thus he never identified the suspect. We would have to rely on William to make the identification. Still, I was confident that a jury would look past these minor holes in our case and put the pieces to the puzzle together.

The Trial

The day of trial, David looked like he was on his deathbed. The flu had taken its toll on him and I wasn't sure he would even make it to court the day of trial. I was prepared to try the case myself if I had to. I was confident I could handle things alone though I knew I would be better off with David's assistance. We hadn't heard from Patricia yet, so we weren't 100% sure we were even going to trial. I looked over my shoulder and saw David slowly staggering towards the front of the court. The judge had taken the bench with all parties present.

"Government, are you ready to proceed with trial?" the Judge asked.

"David Johnson for the government your honor, we are ready to proceed however we extended a plea offer to the defense last night, and ..."

"Your honor my client is rejecting the plea offer and we are ready for trial," Patricia interjected.

"In that case, we are ready for trial your honor," David said.

It was settled; we were in trial. I had practiced my opening statement ad nauseam the night before trial combing over every detail and practicing the right inflections in my voice during my delivery. It was clear that David was only present for moral support. He could barely keep his head out of his hands as we sat at our table. Despite his suffering, he managed to organize the files and offer advice concerning the pretrial motions. One of the issues that arose during pretrial motions was whether we could use the entirety of the 911 call under the Excited Utterance Exception to the general prohibition against introducing hearsay in court. Part of the call was clearly admissible as a statement of identification, but Patricia objected to the portion that included a description of the gun. David had recently tried a case with the same issue and immediately whispered to me that I should argue the gun was also admissible as a part of the description of the suspect. The court accepted our argument and allowed the entirety of the 911 call in as evidence. It was an early victory for us and infuriated Patricia. It didn't take long for her calm demeanor to turn fiercely adversarial when the trial began. The gloves were off, and I was ready for war.

My opening statement went exactly as I had practiced. I felt that I had captivated the jury with William's story while adequately vilifying Tim in the process. I portrayed William as a young entrepreneur looking to earn an honest living in contrast to Tim's criminal opportunism. I smiled as I completed my opening and looked towards David for approval. When our eyes met, I didn't receive the glaring endorsement I expected. I wasn't sure if the flu impacted David's reaction or if my own overconfidence clouded my judgment.

The custodian of records from T-Mobile served as our first witness. I decided that we would put him on first and get the phone records in before starting our case. It was my first time introducing phone logs into the record and everyone in the court could tell. I had clearly underestimated the preparation involved in admitting phone records. I riddled off a bunch of questions for the custodian that appeared to confuse and bore the jury and failed to present the important numbers, dates, and times in a memorable way. The direct examination took too long, and I could sense that after five minutes no one in the courtroom had listened to anything that the witness said. When I finished, I walked back to the table disappointed. I knew that whatever luster I imagined my opening statement had produced was slowly slipping away after our first witness. Nevertheless, I remained hopeful that William would shore up any doubts about our evidence and that I could clean up the poor showing in closings. Patricia could sense that I had dropped the ball and left the stinger in the wound by not asking our witness any questions after my direct. The day ended on a solemn note and David and I walked back to the office in silence rethinking our strategy moving forward.

The next day David texted and notified me that he was bed-ridden and would not be able to make the rest of the trial. A few days ago, I would have received this information in stride, but after the previous day's performance, my confidence had taken a hit. I realized how important David's presence and advice were when I found myself spiraling. Before I knew it, I was back in court alone with William next up to the stand. When I turned to walk towards the witness room, I noticed a group of five young men sitting in the back row. These young men had not been present throughout any of the hearings. It was the middle of the day and no one else was in the courtroom except the parties, the jury, the courtroom employ-ees and these five young men. Tim often peaked over his shoulder in their direction seemingly confirming their presence throughout the morning. When William entered the courtroom, he and I both glanced over at the young men and I could not help but notice their menacing looks and folded arms. At that moment, I began to consider the implications that testifying in court might have on William. He lived not far from where the incident occurred and was known in the community for his work with Big Rod. Justified or not, the neighborhood would label him a snitch, not only for identifying Tim in the robbery but suggesting that Rod had a hand in the conspiracy. William stood about 5'9 weighing 170 lbs. and practiced Buddhism. He was not a violent person and I doubted his ability to defend himself even if he had to. When he took the stand, I noticed a shyness that I had not witnessed in him in our meetings in my office. Previously, he projected an air of confidence that I admired, but today he slumped in his seat and fidgeted as if he had to use the restroom. I started to imagine what it must have felt like to describe a crime in a room with several strangers while sitting directly across from the man who you believed pulled a gun in your face and threatened to shoot you. All the while, watching a group of young men sitting in the back who were likely Rod or Tim's hitmen. When I asked him questions, he often mumbled which prompted the judge to ask that he sit closer to the microphone and speak more clearly. In other trials, I had witnesses look directly at the jury when telling their story. In fact, I tried to position myself in a way that would force the witness to focus on the jury and not me while providing their account of what happened. It made the witness appear more believable and personable. Not William. His eyes were locked on mine the entire direct-examination. My familiar face became the only crutch available to assuage the obvious discomfort that he felt testifying in front of a group of foreigners.

To make matters worse, Patricia objected to my line of questioning at every turn. If I asked an open-ended question and William provided more than a yes or no answer, Patricia would object on the putative grounds that the question called for a narrative. If I asked a direct question, she objected on leading grounds. The defense-friendly judge happily sustained several of the objections. Even when she didn't sustain the request, the objection itself often threw William off track making it difficult for him to get in a flow while testifying. The obstructionist tactic worked. I watched the jury's frustration with our constant visits to the bench to argue the objections. When we got to the point in the story where William described Rod's conversation with his associates about seeing Tim at the community center, Patricia objected on hearsay grounds. She stated that William could not testify about the conversations between the two associates because the statements were out of court statements being offered for their truth, i.e. hearsay. I tried to argue that these were statements of identification, but the judge sustained Patricia's objection. The exclusion represented yet another blow to our case; I wanted the jury to draw the connection between Rod's knowledge of Tim's presence at the community center and his eventual presence at the crime scene, but when the judge excluded the testimony I was deflated. My case kept getting worse by the minute, but I soon realized that the worst was yet to come.

"William, describe the person who robbed you that day," I said.

126

A sudden silence fell upon the courtroom. William stared into his lap thinking about his response. When he lifted his head, I could see him staring over my shoulder at the young men we passed when we entered the courtroom.

"He had long dreads, he was light skinned, but I really couldn't see his face. His dreads were kind of covering his face, so it was hard to see."

I tried to hide my shock. Throughout the entire investigation, William was nothing short of 100% sure that the person who robbed him was the same person he saw in the music videos. I listened as William's credibility diminished right before my eyes. My confident demeanor belied the sinking feeling in my stomach that I had experienced from his testimony. On cross-examination Patricia seized on William's diffidence by confusing him with questions in rapid succession and drilling him on his lack of confidence. When he left the stand, it was clear that our case wasn't as sound as I had previously predicted. After I put Reggie and the detective on the stand, I rested my case. At this point, I knew that I had to expose Rod on the stand as a liar to have any chance at winning. If I could depict Rod as an untrustworthy conspirator in the robbery, I could save our trial from the nose dive it had taken.

We rested our case and, as expected, Patricia called her only witness to the stand, Big Rod. The marshals summoned the guards to bring him from the back. He stepped forward clad in an orange prison jumpsuit chained by the wrist and feet. He had been in prison for only a year, but he had aged three times that number. His former boyish clean face had been replaced by a grizzly beard and a soulless countenance. Patricia started her direct examination.

"Roderick, could you state your name for the jury?" she said.

"Roderick Parker."

"Do you remember shooting a video near the Community Center on Riggs Rd back in May 2015?"

"Yes."

"What happened that day?" asked Patricia.

"Objection your honor, calls for a narrative," I stated.

I figured I would give Patricia a dose of her own medicine, even though I knew the judge wouldn't take kindly to my obvious tit-for-tat pettiness.

"Overruled, you may proceed Mr. Parker," the judge stated as she rolled her eyes in my direction.

"We were shooting a video and we got robbed," responded Rod.

"Did you get a chance to see the person who robbed you?"

"Yes."

"Is that person in the courtroom today?"

"No."

"Do you know Tim Jones?"

"Yes."

"How do you know Tim Jones?"

"From around the way in the neighborhood."

"Did Tim Jones rob you that day back in May 2015?"

"No."

"Rod, I see that you are in an orange jumpsuit. Why don't you tell the jury why you are wearing that jumpsuit."

"Because I shot the person who robbed me that day."

"Objection your honor!" I shouted.

It took me a few minutes to collect my thoughts. I walked to the bench and pled my case to the judge.

"Your honor, I object on relevance grounds," I stated.

"Mr. Jackson, I believe Mr. Parker is stating on the record that he was incarcerated for shooting the person who robbed him," said the judge. "Unless Tim Jones has a bullet wound somewhere on him that we don't know about, I believe this goes directly to his innocence. Overruled."

"No further questions your honor," said Patricia.

I was toast. Patricia had crafted a masterful defense that caught me completely off guard. I needed a moment to collect my thoughts before starting my cross-examination, but I didn't want to look unprepared in front of the jury, so I forged ahead. I played the music video where Rod and Tim embraced.

"This video is about loyalty isn't it, Rod?" I asked.

"Yes," Rod responded.

"You're loyal to your friends, aren't you?" I asked.

"Yes," said Tim.

"And Tim is your friend isn't he. You two look like really good friends on this video, don't you?" I asked.

"Yes," said Tim.

"And you're not a snitch, are you?" I asked.

"No."

"In fact, you would never snitch on Tim even if he was the one who committed this robbery. Isn't that right?" I repeated.

"Yes."

I continued my onslaught for a few more minutes but thinking of questions to rebut his story on the fly proved difficult. In the end, I completed my cross-examination woefully short of impeaching Rod. Quite the contrary, he came across much more credible than I expected a convicted felon serving a ten-year sentence to appear. Patricia rested her case and the jury left the courtroom. I sat at my table for a while thinking about how crucial David's presence would have been during cross. I was not prepared to handle the case alone and I felt the heavy weight of humility pressing upon my ego.

That night I wrecked my brain trying to construct my closing argument. Low on confidence, I struggled to find the right words to fix the many holes in our sinking ship. Twenty-four hours later, I arrived in court nervous and happy at the same time. Nervous about my closing statement and happy the defense would soon put me out of my misery. I had never felt as lonely as I did sitting in that courtroom every day and I wanted it to end. I delivered a lukewarm closing statement. Patricia on the other hand put on a show and even referenced a line from a Bill Murray film at the end of her statement that left the entire jury smiling. It took them less than a day to acquit Tim. When they came back with the verdict, Tim looked in my direction and laughed. I knew he had just gotten away with armed robbery not because the justice system had worked the way it should have but because my own ego had allowed him to.

I shuffled back to my office with the bitter taste of defeat fresh on my mind. I texted David the results and he gave me a feel-good response about moving on to the next case, though I knew in the back of his mind he felt validation. I sat in my office for an hour thinking about everything that went wrong. Still brooding over the loss, I decided to email my assistant to pull Rod's attempted murder case. I had failed to review the case prior to trial not thinking it would have much relevance. I reviewed the statement Rod gave to the officer responsible for writing up his sentencing report. The statement would be informative because it was a defendant's opportunity to explain to the court their remorse for the crime committed. I wrapped my head in my hands as I read the file. Rod had not shot the person who robbed him at all. Quite the contrary, he had shot a random person because he was hard up for cash and needed some money to support himself. Rod had lied on the stand and had I simply requested a recess, I would have been able to call the sentencing officer in my rebuttal case to exploit Rod's perjury.

Had Tim taken the plea to Robbery, William may have received a sense of closure and Tim an acceptance of responsibility. Truthfully, this had always been the best result and I knew it. Ironically, Tim Jones' case marked my final jury trial as a prosecutor. It stuck with me not only for that reason but for the lesson I learned about the importance of separating your needs for validation, notoriety, and self-gratification from your duties as a prosecutor. Otherwise, justice becomes the biggest casualty of war.

7

TO THE VICTOR, GO THE SPOILS

"I'm drunk as shit right now! Gurrrrl, let's go get something to eat." said Keisha.

"You riding with me or Danielle?" said Jessica.

"Bitch, I'm riding wit my sister, you know that," said Keisha.

"Keisha! Gurl you drunk, let's just stop some place and get burgers to go." said Danielle.

It was 3:00 a.m. on a Saturday in Washington, D.C., Keisha, her sister Danielle, their cousin Jessica, and two of Keisha's close friends had just left a club on U Street. The group consumed several shots of liquor before leaving the club and needed food to balance their intoxication before heading back to Maryland. They jumped in two separate cars and drove west on U Street until it turned into Florida and Connecticut. The group decided to stop by the Burger Shop to grab some food to go. When they pulled into the parking lot, they realized there was no drive-through and decided to go inside.

Travis Green stood outside patrolling the restaurant as the girls entered. Green worked as a lieutenant for the D.C. Police department but moonlighted as a security guard for the restaurant on Friday's and Saturday's. During weekends, the restaurant attracted more homeless loiterers than usual, and Lt. Green served as an effective deterrent. He noticed that the group of young women were loud and play fighting in the parking lot. Green made his presence known by opening the door for them as they entered the restaurant cursing loudly. When the door closed behind them, he peeked into the store for a few seconds to see if their commotion escalated into anything worth his attention. Their boisterousness continued inside the restaurant but nothing warranting Lt. Green to ask the five young women to leave the store.

Justin was present with his night crew. After six months of night shifts, his team had grown accustomed to the type of customers the shift drew. Many of the patrons were drunk or homeless people looking for a free meal and shelter. Some of them were disrespectful causing Justin to summon Lt. Green to escort them out. But for the most part, the customers didn't bother Justin; he was more focused on the night staff whose company he enjoyed. They were loyal to him and he had built close relationships with each employee. The crew of four included Tasha, James, Joyce and Lisa. Tasha had started around the same time as Justin and the two became friends over the years. When Justin became manager, he hired James, Joyce and Lisa to join his team. The crew worked well together and often spent time with each other outside of work.

Justin had been working at the Burger Shop on Connecticut Avenue for five years. He started out as a part-time line-cook during high school and went full time after his senior year. He lacked the grades and the finances to attend college, but he did possess natural leadership qualities. Sam Young, Burger Shop's regional manager, recognized this when the manager at the time took leave for a family emergency. Justin took over in her absence and Sam noticed how well he ran the restaurant. Justin was soft spoken but possessed a magnetic sense of humor. He also had a reputation amongst his colleagues for reliability and fairness. Justin would often work double shifts for team members who needed to call in sick; he would come in on his days off to help the restaurant during busy hours. Sam recognized Justin's potential and promoted him to manager after his second year at the restaurant. For Justin, the money couldn't have come at a better time. Justin's mother and father had passed when he was five years old. His grandmother raised him up until the day she passed during Justin's senior year of high school. Without much family support, he bounced from couch to couch hoping to save up for his own place. With the significant increase in salary, he could finally afford it. The promotion changed the trajectory of Justin's life from a man struggling with poverty and teetering on the edge of homelessness to a decent wage earner able to pay his bills.

Justin monitored the number of orders pending on the screen when he heard commotion coming from the entrance. He turned to observe Keisha and her crew entering the store with Lt. Green holding open the door. Danielle approached the line first with Keisha, Jessica, and their two friends closely behind. Joyce stood behind the counter taking orders, but the malfunctioning register held up the line. This began to upset Keisha's crew as they grew restless in line. In a drunken playful mood, Danielle picked up a yellow caution sign that covered a wet spot on the floor and swung it at Keisha.

"Ok bitch, you want to play now huh!" said Keisha, as she charged at Danielle as if she would land a right cross.

"Put that cone down please. That's not a play toy," warned Justin.

Daniele dropped the cone on the floor and flashed a look of disdain towards Justin.

"Where is our fucking food man? We've been waiting on our damn order for fifteen minutes," said Keisha.

"Your order is on the way, but yall are doing too much in this line and disturbing customers," said Justin. "If you can't keep your hands to yourself and stay in line, I'm going to have to ask you to leave."

"We're not going any fucking where without our food," said Danielle.

At this point, Justin noticed other customers leaving the store without making orders. Only two young women remained near the cash register patiently awaiting their orders but becoming annoyed with the belligerent cast of girls. Anticipating further commotion, Lisa had crept out the back door and informed Lt. Green that he should come inside. When Lt. Green entered, he saw Danielle and Keisha both yelling at Justin.

"That's why you're working at this shitty fast food place anyway-big nose ass!" screamed Keisha.

Justin gave Lt. Green the signal that the store would no longer serve the group.

"Girls, I'm going to have to ask you to leave," stated Lt. Green calmly.

Emboldened by the presence of Lt. Green, the two customers who were previously waiting silently for their food began to comment on the buffoonery.

"Y'all too old to be acting like some little kids," said one customer.

Danielle immediately sprung forward and began a shouting match with the two female customers. Lt. Green struggled to keep the two separated as Danielle circled around him attempting to gain position on her target. On the other side of the counter, Justin continued preparing the girl's order in hopes that giving them their bags would neutralize the situation. Instead, Keisha picked up the vanilla shake that Justin prepared and hurled it towards Justin's face dashing him in the eyes.

Justin had seen enough. He grabbed a fist full of paper towels and scrubbed his face. He charged towards the door leading from behind the counter to the area open to customers.

"Lt. Green, it's time for these girls to go. Get them out the door, now." Yelled Justin.

When Keisha saw Justin had come from behind the counter, she approached him getting close enough for the two to touch foreheads. Then, before Justin could react, Keisha collected a ball of spit in her throat and shot a projectile of saliva right into Justin's face. Justin immediately pushed her back out of his face and in seconds found himself surrounded by Keisha, Danielle, and Jessica with his back to the wall. Justin was 6'2 and 210 lbs. of pure muscle. He was no stranger to the gym and spent a lot of time lifting weights. He knew he could have easily taken them all, but he heeded his grandmother's words to never to hit women and restrained himself. As he retreated backwards, the five girls continued to curse at him and make threats as they closed in. Suddenly, Keisha's friend, Lauren, threw her milkshake at Justin making it the second to connect on his face that night. And from that point, all hell broke loose. The girls attacked Justin as he tried to smoosh them in the face without throwing punches. Staff members intervened as an all-out brawl ensued.

Justin covered his head as he took punches from all angles. Lt. Green attempted to separate the group with his long wingspan. The fighting displaced the island in the middle of the restaurant holding the ketchup, mustard and other condiments. It now rested closer to the door on the side where Keisha and her group held their ground. Keisha, in a drunken rage, grabbed a glass vinegar bottle from the island and hurled it at the group striking Justin flush in the face, breaking his nose. Danielle, equally enraged, picked up a metal pole partitioning the customer line and flung it across the room narrowly missing Joyce. Keisha threw another bottle, this one struck Justin in the back of his head opening a six-inch gash under his dreadlocks. Noticing the level of violence had ramped up, Justin, Lt. Green and James began to impose their physical strength on the group and pressed them closer to the restaurant door. Lt. Green had called for back-up and didn't want the group to escape so he found himself attempting to keep the group inside until reinforcements came, inversely the staff fought to get them out.

When the blue lights finally arrived, the police separated the groups. Officers placed Keisha, Jessica, and Danielle in police vans.

Justin had suffered a broken nose and visited the hospital to receive staples to close the back of his head. Joyce had suffered a broken thumb and sustained lacerations to her neck. The restaurant was a total disaster with bottles, poles, chairs, and miscellaneous objects strewn everywhere-Lt. Green described it to his fellow officers eloquently: "fifteen minutes of pure hell".

War

Two years later, a colleague and close friend, Travis, stopped by my office with a file. I had just moved up to felony major crimes and he was on his way to prosecuting major narcotics trafficking. He needed to divvy out his felony cases before leaving and, given our friendship, he wanted to give me a slam dunk case to begin my new rotation. Travis had already indicted the case and done most of the leg work. All I needed to do was prep the witnesses and tighten up loose ends. I took the file and thanked him. That evening I kicked my feet up and peeled through the evidence. I came across a sleeve with a DVD inside; it was the surveillance video from the Burger Shop. The video depicted the entire incident. I reared back in my chair with mixed emotions thinking to myself: these girls are toast.

Being a black male prosecutor bore striking similarities to serving as a black male overseer during slavery. Of course, key differences existed; unlike overseers, we weren't born as prosecutors or required to take the job nor were we purchased at an auction, but certain unfortunate parallels existed. Most, if not all, of the people who we prosecuted were black and poor. Many of them were born into a virtually inescapable system designed to keep them confined until death. Many of us had family members or friends who were trapped in or impacted by the very system that we were helping to enforce. Many of us viewed acceptance of our roles as preferable to having no power to determine our sister's and brother's fates.

Never in my wildest dreams did I imagine myself one day work-ing with police to send people to prison. Seeing my future self in the courtroom advocating for a black man or woman to go to jail would have been like Malcom X, after his prison stint, envisioning himself marrying a white woman, or Angela Davis sporting a weave. In the neighborhood I grew up in, the criminal justice system and everyone who played a part in it was the enemy. The police, the judge, and certainly the prosecutor were all intent on locking black men and women up and throwing away the figurative key without a flinch. Even defense attorneys couldn't be trusted, because I assumed money and plea bargains motivated them. The historical relationship between the criminal justice system and African Americans justified this paranoia and my experiences as a black man in my own community solidified it.

I recall my excitement at eighteen when my father purchased my first car. I also remember the concerned look on his face after he handed me the keys. It didn't take long for me to understand at least part of the source of his trepidation. Within three weeks of owning my first car, the police had already pulled me over several times for random traffic violations. One cop saw it fit to order me out of the car and frisk me in front of my vehicle; I guess failing to signal before changing lanes provided sufficient suspicion of me carrying a weapon. And of course, there was my all-expense paid visit to Florida jail for suspicion of DUI which only turned out to be a valid suspicion of driving while black. I recall stories about judges too—whether it was hefty sentences for minor offenses or outrageous child support orders for men with no possible means of paying. Judges would then turn around and put them in jail for contempt when they failed to pay. And at the center of the web of injustice lied the prosecutor. The *sine qua non* of the black criminal justice experience—a person thought to be hell bent on securing a conviction irrespective of innocence or guilt.

While in law school, I studied the Constitution and its relation to Criminal Law and Criminal Procedure. In my limited free time, I read books about Charles Hamilton Houston and Thurgood Marshall and earned a new-found respect for defense attorneys. I began to develop a more sophisticated understanding of the intricacies of the system but reading opinions such as *Scott v. Sanford* and *Plessy v. Ferguson* only cemented my cynical outlook that outcomes in the criminal justice system have been and continue to be based on the agendas of lawmakers and not necessarily principles of fairness. And it wasn't just those old overruled cases that are now viewed as relics of past racism that caught my attention. Lesser known cases (outside of the legal community) such as *Terry v. Ohio* and its progeny, which permit the police to stop citizens on "reasonable suspicion" of criminal conduct, troubled me as well. I finally understood how the police were able to legally harass so many people in my old neighborhood on a regular basis. Reasonable suspicion was as subjective as it sounded, and the police applied the concept disparately against people of color in poor neighborhoods. I also learned that the probable cause standard required prior to an arrest could be overcome by something as unreliable as a statement from a bitter ex-lover or a nosey neighbor. You could be locked away based solely on the unsubstantiated claim of one witness; many times that witness was a police officer. The police could obtain a warrant, raid your home, and go on a treasure hunt based on the statements of one officer.

I learned a great deal about the power of the prosecutor in my federal criminal law class. My professor was a former federal prosecutor and defense attorney. He had spent the first part of his career prosecuting major drug offenses and then moved up to homicide. After many years as a prosecutor, he decided to flip and dedicate the remainder of his career to criminal appeals. He was a demanding professor who often assigned hundreds of pages of reading between classes and quizzed us on each of the cases in class. Embarrassment often befell the unprepared; he would lash out at anyone who clearly had not read the cases he assigned, which kept the small class on its toes. We had heated debates about sentencing guidelines, RICO laws, and most importantly prosecutorial discretion. That discretion, I learned, is what makes the prosecutor the most powerful person in the criminal justice system. I began to rethink my views about the prospect of becoming a prosecutor. Although, I remained a skeptic of the system, I began to envision how incarceration rates might change if the demographics of DA offices across the country also changed. I thought about Thurgood Marshall's experience defending the Groveland Boys and how different it might have been if a black prosecutor stood on the other side of the isle. Would the Groveland Boys still have needed Marshall's services? I also reflected on Johnnie Cochran's stint as a DA in Los Angeles and how he used the trial experience to develop his abilities early in his career. The prospect of becoming a prosecutor became less repulsive to me; in fact, I began to view the position as an opportunity to influence the system in a way that combated racism while gaining career propelling trial experience.

My vision of becoming a system upending prosecutor hadn't exactly panned out as I had planned. A month before the Burger Shop trial I found myself faced with a familiar dilemma. I wanted to give Keisha, Danielle and Jessica a break. We had charged Keisha and Danielle both with Assault with a Dangerous Weapon for throwing the bottle and the pole respectively. The felony carried up to ten years in prison. Keisha was also charged with Felony Assault for the injuries Justin received to his nose and head. The surveillance footage, which showed the entire incident from beginning to end, depicted Danielle assisting her friends by striking Justin on the back of the head with a closed fist, so we only charged her with misdemeanor assault.

Despite the severity of Justin's injuries and the wanton actions of the three girls, I had no desire to convict these young women. Only Keisha had a record, a single offense for assault several years ago. Jessica and Danielle had never been charged with a crime in their adult lives. Jessica was a college student at a local university with a major in accounting; I knew a conviction would damage her future job prospects. Keisha was a single mother raising a 5-year-old daughter on a modest hourly wage from a job that she had just started a month ago. A conviction for Keisha might mean losing her only means of providing for her child. Danielle was currently unemployed but had hopes of enrolling in cosmetology classes in the fall. A conviction for her might mean that she could never hold a license as a cosmetologist. If the decision were completely my own, I would have offered the three of them a deferred prosecution agreement requiring them to write Justin a letter of apology, pay for his medical bills, and participate in community service. Had they completed the terms of the agreement, they would be free to go with no criminal record. Unfortunately, I knew the unlikelihood of finding a supervisor to approve a deferred prosecution in an indicted felony case. Moreover, on a personal level I wanted the trial experience. Significant trial numbers led to promotions. No career defining incentive existed to plea cases out, especially slam dunk cases like the one Travis had given me. After ten minutes of thinking, I sat back in my chair and kicked my feet up near my keyboard and took a deep breath. I picked up the Burger Shop case file and searched for the attorneys' numbers.

"Hello," said Keisha's attorney, Mrs. Jones.

"Mrs. Jones, this is Martinis Jackson, with the U.S. Attorney's office. I want to discuss a potential resolution of this case. We cannot give you a deferred prosecution agreement, but we can give your client two misdemeanors charges for assault and one charge for unlawful entry," I said.

"Mr. Jackson, my client is not interested in a guilty plea that would result in a criminal record," said Mrs. Jones.

"Mrs. Jones, this case is not going to be a difficult case to prove. Have you seen the surveillance video? This is your client's final chance to avoid a felony conviction. I will give you until the end of the week to accept the offer," I said.

"It was nice speaking with you Mr. Jackson," she replied.

I had similar conversations with Danielle and Jessica's attorneys. I was shocked to hear their responses. It was clear that either they had not reviewed the evidence, or their clients did not understand the case mounted against them. We not only had surveillance video footage, but we had an off-duty police officer on scene who witnessed the entire incident. We had medical records, photos of injuries and several witnesses from the Burger Shop who corroborated our narrative. None of our witnesses had criminal records and none of them knew the defendants, so there was no issue with bias. Whatever the reason the three of them believed they could beat this case, it was out of my hands at that point.

It was June 15, 2016 and I was seated to the left of my trial partner and close friend, Lisa. The judge excluded the exhibit I intended to use for my opening statement – a photo of Justin's broken nose – which agitated me. I caressed my tie while staring into the patterns, thinking through my statement while listening to the judge address the jury. I could see the three defendants staring at me and Lisa with menacing eyes from behind the defense table. My supervisor sat quietly in the back row awaiting my opening statement in a courtroom filled with other attorneys and defendants awaiting hearings. I felt the nervousness that I always felt before giving a statement in front of fourteen unfamiliar faces. Anyone who knows me knows that I hate speaking in public, it is one of my biggest fears. In high school and undergrad, I often experienced panic attacks when I had to give a presentation or offer my opinion in front of classmates. To overcome my fears, I joined Toastmasters before I attended law school to develop my public speaking skills and to muster the courage to face my fears. With that experience, I realized that although I struggled on my feet, I could memorize anything. This was a skill I developed at a young age while competing in bible study quizzes that required me to commit to memory entire chapters of the bible and recite them on command. I had also become accustomed to committing things to memory during my brief music career for performances on stage. When I started to write my speeches out and commit them to memory, I immediately saw my confidence and effectiveness increase.

"Mr. Jackson, you may address the jury," said the judge.

I had gone over the opening statement repeatedly in my head and when I stood up it rolled off my tongue like a familiar song. I could tell the jury was eating out of my hands as each person's eyes never lost contact with mine. Even the judge watched my every movement. I gestured towards the defendants during one part of my statement, pointing an accusatory finger in their direction. I noticed the fearful look in their eyes. They knew that they had made a mistake. Their attorneys shared the look of disdain as all three of their faces cringed. When I finished, I turned to walk back to my seat and noticed a smile on both Lisa and my supervisor's face. It was now time for the defense attorneys to give their openings. Their performances were subpar to say the least. Both fumbled through the facts and failed to offer compelling reasons to acquit their clients. A quick glance at the defendants and you could see them sinking slowly in their seats likely wishing they could reconsider the plea agreement.

The trial lasted three days and despite a few hiccups along the way (Lt. Green lying about a civil complaint and Justin appearing late for court) we knew the video showed enough to convict. To make matters worse for the defendants, Justin came across as an honest and sympathetic witness who worked hard to earn a living only to be disrespected by the defendants that night. Lisa gave a closing statement as equally compelling as my opening. Although the defense attorneys performed better in closings, we knew their arguments wouldn't be enough. The jury only had about thirty minutes left in the day to deliberate so the judge sent them home for the evening to return in the morning and begin deliberations fresh. It was the judge, however who would pass judgment on Jessica, because she only faced a misdemeanor charge. We figured the case against her was the strongest given the clear evidence of her striking Justin on camera. For the judge to acquit, he would need to accept the defense-of-others theory that all three defendants presented. The judge would have to find that Jessica was not only protecting her friends when she attacked Justin but that her friends were justified in attacking Justin first, which was clearly not the case.

The judge swiftly ran through his findings and found Jessica guilty of misdemeanor assault and unlawful entry. Jessica's face filled with disappointment, a demeanor opposite that of her attorney's, who had long accepted defeat. It was Jessica's first offense and she was facing 180 days in prison but there was no way we would ask for that much time. In fact, I wasn't planning on asking for any jail time at all. I simply wanted Jessica to pay for Justin's medical bills and stay away from the Burger Shop. Since Justin could not attend Jessica's verdict, the judge postponed sentencing until we afforded him an opportunity to speak to the court about his views on punishment. Typically, the law favors release over imprisonment pending trial, unless the defendant is accused of a violent crime, has a violent history, or is a flight risk. However, this presumption is reversed once a defendant is found guilty of a crime, there is an inherent risk of flight, but usually for first offenders convicted of misdemeanors, the presumption is easily overcome, and the defendant is set free until sentencing. Unfortunately for Jessica, she became the exception to the rule.

"Alright, since we don't have the victim here with a statement. We will have to set sentencing out a few weeks from now," said the judge. "In the meanwhile, marshals please step the defendant back to jail pending sentencing."

The room fell silent with disbelief. A look of panic fell over the face of Jessica who was likely told there was no way she would visit a prison for this offense. Keisha and Danielle looked equally horrified as they undoubtedly began to ponder their fates.

"Your honor! My client has no prior record at all. She is not a flight risk or a danger to the community! We ask that you reconsider," Jessica's attorney exclaimed.

"Marshals step her back," the judge said nonchalantly. "Anything else counsel?"

When I watched the marshals take her away, I could see her eyes swell with tears. Her friends were already shedding tears. Jessica had only been convicted of a misdemeanor and faced jail time—what should they expect? The entire trial the three exhibited stoic demeanors, but that façade quickly disappeared when the prospect of prison became a reality. When I glanced over at Keisha and Danielle, they stared back with a look of disbelief. It was the look I had seen in the eyes of many defendants in the face of imminent defeat, a look I can never erase from memory. If those eyes had a voice, they would say:

Black man, how could you send me to jail?
How could you contribute to a system that targets us both?
In another life, we may have been close friends, brothers,
or partners. We share the same enemy, do we not?

My face sunk into the floor with regret, but I should have anticipated the judge's response. He was also a black man and notorious for teaching defendants a lesson, especially young defendants. This wasn't the first time he had sent one of my defendants to jail unexpectedly. In a misdemeanor trial that I won a year prior, he sentenced an 18-year-old first offender to thirty days in jail for beating up his father in a self-described effort to teach the young man a lesson about respecting his parents. I knew that he only intended to send a similar message to the young girls about respect. I doubted that Jessica would serve more than a few weeks in jail. Besides, Justin and his crew were the real victims here. Jessica had brought this upon herself; she would learn the hard way, but she needed to learn. These were the things I told myself to justify my participation in Jessica's incarceration but none of it worked. Deep down inside I knew that locking Jessica away in a cage served no purpose. It simply reflected the limited tools our criminal justice system used to deter criminal behavior.

The next day, Keisha and Danielle returned to court visibly nervous about their anticipated verdicts. Keisha had brought her daughter to court with her for the first time during the trial. I had seen this strategy before, defendants would bring family and friends, especially children, in hopes of persuading the judge not to lock them up.

"Make sure all children have caretakers present in the event of a guilty verdict in this case," the judge noted.

The jury had submitted a note to the judge asking a question about the charges. This gave the defense hope that there might be confusion among the jury pool and a potential acquittal or hung jury. The note posed a legal question that both sides argued about for a while before the judge made a final ruling. The clerk sent back the judge's response to the jury in letter form. We were told that chambers would contact both parties if the jury reached a verdict. Lisa and I packed up our bags and walked out of the courtroom. Trials were always draining, and we were both weary from the emotional roller coaster we endured over the past few days. We discussed the jury note and speculated about the jury's thought process. Were they having doubts? What could we have done better? Suddenly, I felt a vibration on the right side of my leg; it was my work phone. When I saw the area code and number, I knew it was the Judge's chambers.

"Mr. Jackson, we have a verdict. Please come back," said the clerk.

"We will be right there," I said.

We both turned around and hurried back to the courtroom. We didn't say much on the way back as both of us were consumed by our own thoughts. When we arrived, Keisha and Danielle were already waiting with their attorneys seated at the defense table. The judge and clerks were present awaiting our arrival.

"The jury says that they have reached a verdict. Mr. Bailey would you please go and escort the jury in please," said the judge.

Ms. Bailey, the court's clerk, went back into the deliberation room and returned within seconds with the twelve jurors behind her. As they entered, we stood and waited for them to be seated before we took our seats.

"I received a note that the jury has reached a verdict. Is that correct?" said the judge.

"Yes, your honor," said the foreperson.

"Please bring the verdict forward," said the judge.

The foreperson was juror number 4, an older black woman who was retired from teaching. I remembered liking her during *voir dire* because she had a no nonsense look on her face as she came forward. I also knew older people would sympathize with our theme of respect and decency. She handed Ms. Bailey the verdict slip, and Ms. Bailey handed it to the judge. He surveyed the verdict swiftly and, without expression, returned it to Ms. Bailey who then gave it back to the foreperson.

"Alright, as to Danielle Bowen and the charge of Assault with a Dangerous Weapon, how does the jury find Ms. Bowen?"

"Guilty, your honor," said the foreperson.

"As to the charge of Felony Assault against Keisha Bowen, how does the jury find Ms. Bowen?"

"Guilty your honor," she said again.

I stared forward during the guilty verdict, not looking in the eyes of the judge or the jury. For me, a guilty verdict made me think back to my federal criminal law professor's words about the difference between being a prosecutor and a defense attorney. He would say "I never felt good about hearing a guilty verdict as a prosecutor, it only meant that the trial was over and I hadn't loss, but when I was a defense attorney and my client was cleared of guilt that was one of the greatest feelings in the world." I imagined that, at that moment, Keisha and Danielle were experiencing the worst feelings in the world. The jury came back guilty on all counts. When they were excused, we all rose, and I finally looked towards the jury right as they walked out of the door. The juror sitting nearest to my seat looked me in my eyes and nodded once as if to say, "job well done."

As expected, despite Keisha and Danielle's attorney's many pleas, the judge stepped them both back to jail to await their sentencing dates which were over a month away. The two were now felons and would spend forty days in jail before sentencing. In the blink of an eye, their lives had changed forever.

Justin appeared for Jessica's sentencing and gave his victim impact statement. He had recently been fired from the Burger Shop due to his increased absences that resulted from the migraine headaches he experienced after the blow to his head. He was jobless again and could no longer afford his apartment, finding himself back on the streets. Despite his downward spiral, he explained to the court that he didn't want to see Danielle, Keisha or Jessica do jail time. He only wanted his medical expenses paid for and to move on with his life. The judge let Jessica go and ordered her to pay one-third of Justin's medical fees while placing her on a year of probation. Keisha and Danielle were given the same order and were released after a month and a half of jail.

I often thought about what became of Justin, Danielle, Keisha and Jessica. The criminal justice system had worked the way many believed it should, yet I doubted anyone was any better off because of it. Keisha and Danielle would wear the badge of felon for much of their lives, closing them off from opportunities to become productive citizens. Jessica walked away with a misdemeanor, though not as damaging as a felony, it came with its own collateral consequences. Justin lost his job and would have to wait years for the appellate process to end and even more time before the prospect of any restitution came to fruition.

With each conviction, I knew I was fighting the wrong battle. There were no winners in the adversarial system, the most you could hope for was a victim receiving some semblance of recompense from a guilty defendant who acknowledged wrongdoing without incurring the lifelong consequences of a felony. Such was the result I had hoped for in this case; but instead I was left with yet another pyrrhic victory.

8

FAMILY MATTERS

James had been working for metro transit for a year as a technician. His job duties consisted of visiting metro stops within his service area and conducting maintenance on the tracks. Technicians typically worked in units of two, so James often worked with Tim, an older technician with whom he quickly became close friends. The two shared stories during their rides together.

It was a humid summer day in Northeast D.C., near the Rhode Island Avenue metro; James and Tim were taking their routine lunch break and decided to eat Subway while they sat on the tailgate of their white government issued van. Tim boasted about his conquest of two women he worked with at his part-time job while James chuckled in between bites of his sandwich.

"I had shawty doing whatever I wanted Joe," stated Tim.

"You a fool," James replied with a half-laugh while checking his phone to see if he had received any text messages.

While listening, James began staring over the hill where the two friends were perched. He looked down near the bus stop at a group walking towards the bus bench. Immediately, James rolled up his sandwich in the wrapper, crammed it back into the plastic bag, placed the bag on the end of the tailgate and started walking towards the group. Tim, oblivious to James' movements, continued bragging for a few more minutes until he noticed James half-way down the hill.

"Hey man, where you headed?!" asked Tim.

James didn't answer. He scurried down the hill approaching the group from behind while they stood near the bus bench. The woman, man and two children in the group were all standing waiting on the bus and hadn't noticed James' presence behind them. "What's up?!" exclaimed James.

Tisha turned around first followed by her boyfriend, Eric, and her two sons—Michael and Jeremiah.

"You been keeping my son from me? Why you not answering my calls Tisha?" stated James.

Tisha's face turned pale with fright as she braced herself for what was to come.

Three months later, I was sitting in the witness room right outside of the courtroom talking to James about what happened that day when he walked down the hill and approached the group. I had just picked up the trial a few hours prior to meeting him and knew little to nothing about the case. Trying cases in the misdemeanor domestic violence unit felt like a game of hot potato; cases were passed around from prosecutor to prosecutor and you never knew whose case you might take to trial on any given day. The process required you to learn about the facts of a case, speak to your witnesses, create an opening statement and prepare for trial within an hour or less. Each day you played this game of roulette never knowing what type of trial you might pick up, placing faith in your colleague's preparation of the case file, aka the jacket. Frequently, you had no idea you were having a trial until the judge called your case and asked if the parties were present—a fact well known to the defense bar who took advantage of our lack of preparation at every turn.

"Calling 2016 DV 1000. U.S. v. Latisha Johnson. Parties please state your name for the record," said the Clerk.

"Martinis Jackson, for the United States, your honor," I said.

"Peter Robinson for the Defendant, Ms. Latisha Johnson, who is standing to my left your honor," said the defense.

"Alright, Mr. Jackson, is the prosecution ready to go forward?" stated Judge Bailey.

"May I call out and see if our witness is in the courtroom your honor?" I said.

I saw James raise his hand in the crowd and suddenly I realized that I was about to be in trial. James appeared average height with a slender build and tattoos covering his arms and neck. He wore his yellow government issued vest on top of a tattered gray T-shirt with blue jeans.

Finding male victims in domestic violence cases who actually showed up for trial rarely occurred. Even less common were those who seemed eager about going forward. I sat in the witness room as I listened to James' version of the story just minutes before our trial.

James informed me that two years prior to the incident, he and Tisha had ended their rocky relationship of eight years. When the two met, Tisha had a four-year-old son named Michael and four years into the relationship James and Tisha conceived a child of their own named Jeremiah. James admitted that he wasn't the perfect boyfriend and that arguments and breakups plagued their relationship. In an ideal situation, I would have asked more probing questions but with only a few hours before trial I didn't have the time. James noted that Tisha currently struggled with addiction and depression leaving him to raise their 6-year-old son by himself. Despite her issues, he allowed Tisha to keep Jeremiah every weekend from Friday to Sunday night.

The weekend prior to the incident, Tisha had picked up Jeremiah and told James she would return him on Sunday per their usual arrangement, but when Sunday evening rolled around, and James hadn't heard from Tisha, he began to worry. He knew about Tisha's homelessness. Family members eventually closed their

151

doors due to her alleged addict behaviors. She lived in shelters and sometimes slept at different men's houses throughout the week. On weekends, her family would allow her to stay with them out of love for Jeremiah but would ask her to leave when she returned him. After a day of searching, James turned to bed and hoped he would hear something by the end of the next day, if not, he would call the police.

When James saw his son headed towards the bus the next day, he experienced feelings of relief and rage. Once he made his presence known, he attempted to steer his son away from the group and walk him towards his work van where Tim was located.

"I'm taking my son home with me!" exclaimed James.

At this point, Tisha began screaming at James and punching him in the back of the head while Michael, Jeramiah and Eric looked on. James screamed towards the hill at Tim seeking his help. Fifty feet away, Tim observed the altercation from the top of the hill. As Tisha landed blows to the back of James' head, Eric came around to James' left side and struck him on his left temple knocking James to the ground. Tisha fell to the ground with James as he pulled her down by her shirt. Michael and Eric joined in the fray, kicking and punching James while he covered up on the ground.

We were required to have an officer present during our witness conferences in case the witness changed their story on the stand and we needed the officer to testify to that effect. Present in the witness room that day was Officer Ivanov. He was uniquely qualified for this task because he was sitting in his squad car at the Rhode Island metro that day when he witnessed the scuffle between James and the group from about fifty feet away. James recalls calling out for help to Officer Ivanov when the assault occurred and watching from the ground as Officer Ivanov ran towards the conflict. By the time Officer Ivanov had arrived, Eric had fled the scene and James had gained position on top of Tisha just prior to Officer Ivanov separating them.

After separating the two, Officer Ivanov called for backup and began canvassing the area for Eric—leaving James and Tisha separated by two park benches that were fifteen feet apart. As Officer Ivanov walked away, James turned his attention towards Tisha who had placed a fist-sized rock in a net that she found on the ground. James stood up and watched as Tisha began walking slowly towards him with the net dangling by her side.

"What you think you doing with that?" James said half grinning.

Off in the distance, Ivanov and two other officers had caught up to Eric and were escorting him back to the group. Tim remained just a few feet away from Tisha and James, watching as Tisha got within arm's reach of his coworker. Suddenly, James felt blood running from the middle of his head. When he touched his face, he felt the tenderness of an open gash. Tisha had struck him with a single blow to the forehead. He hadn't remembered the swing, but the impact was unforgettable. Within seconds, Officer Ivanov and other members of MPD had sprinted back to the park and grabbed the rock from Tisha before escorting her to the squad car and transporting her to jail.

James finished his story visibly emotional throughout his rendition. I had James identify the photos in the case file and explain a few additional details before I asked him to wait inside of the courtroom.

"It's something about that guy that makes me think he's not telling the entire story," said Officer Ivanov.

Strangely enough, I felt the same way, but I could not articulate a reason to doubt his claims. The blow to his head left a lasting scar and, if he were a woman, there wouldn't be a question in my mind about pushing for a trial.

After James left the room, I brought in Tim to discuss his version of events. The judge's relatively short calendar meant I only had a few more minutes before trial began. Tim gave me a quick rundown of his version of the story and I checked for glaring inconsistencies. At the tail end of his recollection, I heard a knocking on the door.

"Mr. Jackson, the judge is asking that all parties return for opening statements," said the Judge's Clerk.

Nervousness began to set in. There was no time to draft an opening statement and I could barely remember anything from the witness conferences. When I made my way to the courtroom, I noticed that it was empty aside from the parties to the case, the judge and her clerk.

"Calling 2016 DV 1000, parties please state your name for the record," droned the clerk.

"Martinis Jackson for the prosecution," I said.

"Peter Robinson, for the defendant your honor."

I glanced at my opponent. Certain defense attorneys were notorious within our office for their courtroom antics. If our office ever created a most wanted list of attorneys from the criminal defense bar, Peter Robinson represented Al Capone. He was a tall African-American male in his mid-40s with long dreadlocks. Peter was charismatic and known for gaining the confidence of fledgling prosecutors outside of the courtroom during seemingly innocuous conversations. When he could, he would then turn around and use the substance of those conversations to embarrass his opponent in front of the judge. He also had no problem bending the truth, so his client could beat charges. Judges often berated him for appearing hours late for hearings and seeking continuances for dubious reasons. When I glanced over at him during the trial call, I could see him smiling as if he could smell the milk on my breath as I spoke.

"Your honor, I don't believe we have all of the photos in this case. There is no photo of the rock that was allegedly used to strike the victim in this case," said Robinson.

"Mr. Jackson, what is your response?" said the judge.

The question caught me completely off guard.

"May I have a brief recess your honor," I said.

I took my file to the witness room where Officer Ivanov awaited. In a panicked voice, I asked if he knew the officer who took the photos in the case. We searched through the paperwork and identified the crime scene officer—Officer Green. Officer Ivanov gave him a call to confirm whether he had taken photos of the rock but after several attempts we were unable to reach him. I knew I couldn't go forward with the case without confirming whether the photos existed, so I had no choice but to return to court and inform the judge about the missing evidence.

Mr. Robinson had successfully gained a continuance without much effort. In domestic violence cases, delay served as a defense attorney's best friend and a prosecutor's worst enemy. Each continuance increased the chance of the victim losing interest or being convinced (often by the defense attorney themselves) not to go forward. Each day that passed, our witnesses' memories faded along with the strength of our case. Every day, the court dismissed dozens of cases for the government's failure to present a witness. Although our office could re-bring the case, given the volume of new cases and the burden of starting the process anew, we rarely ever did.

I walked back into court and Peter immediately pulled me to the side to see what I had found. When I relayed the information I received, he smiled as we both approached the bench.

"Mr. Jackson, what were you able to find out about the photos in this case?" said the judge.

"Your honor, we were unable to reach the officer who took the photos in this case, so we are unable to confirm whether or not he took additional photos that the government may be missing. I would request that we move forward as the government has no reason to believe that photos are missing in this case," I replied.

"Your honor, the government is seeking to go forward on a case where photos are clearly missing," stated Peter. "I have it on good information and belief that the crime scene officer took photos of the rock in this case. I would like the opportunity to subpoena the crime scene officer and retrieve the photos myself."

I knew for a fact Peter Robinson was not going to subpoena the officer or search for the photos. He didn't appear prepared for trial and this was an easy way to push the trial back, but I wasn't completely sure my officer hadn't taken photos of the rock. Frankly, I expected to see this type of photo in the jacket as part of the evidence.

"Very well, I will grant the defense's motion to continue. This case will be adjourned 30 days out," the judge noted.

"You know, you should talk to your supervisor about dismissing this case, young blood" Peter whispered as he and Tisha walked past my table, down the walkway and headed towards the exit.

I cracked a condescending smile and ignored his suggestion. Defeated at the hearing, my competitive spirit wouldn't let it go. I explained the court's decision to James and Tim in the witness room and stressed the importance of them attending the next trial date. Both promised to attend, and I quickly went to work searching for an answer to our alleged missing photo question.

Thirty days passed quickly, and I had spent several of them working on dozens of other cases, but I made sure to invest time in James' case. I reached the crime scene officer who acknowledged taking a picture of the rock, but unfortunately, he had no idea where he stored the photo. This was certainly unfortunate news. Although the court would not dismiss my case for this violation, I knew Peter Robinson would have a field day with the missing photo. When I returned to court the next day, my prediction proved accurate.

"Your honor, I move to have this case dismissed," stated Peter. "It is the government's responsibility to preserve evidence in this case and it failed to do so. Who knows what other evidence is missing. The government had thirty days to find this photo and has already shown the court that this is a shoddy investigation. The court should not reward them by allowing this case to move forward."

My blood boiled during Peter's tirade. I expected him to ask for a dismissal, but he took it a step too far by accusing me of conducting a shoddy investigation. I became flustered and I tried to fire back at him by reminding the court that it was the defense who had requested the continuance in the first place to subpoena the officer in the case but hadn't done so. My voice trembled with anger and the court could tell I was losing my composure. The judge ignored my complaints but denied Peter's request.

"I do find that the government violated Rule 16 by failing to provide the defense with the photos upon request; however, I do not find a need for sanctions in this case," the judge stated. "The missing photo of the rock will not prejudice the defense, nor will it determine guilt or innocence and I find that there was no bad faith on the part of the government. If there is nothing further from the defense or the government, government please call your first witness."

Appearing before a government friendly judge paid dividends. Peter went on a tangent for a few more minutes but the judge didn't budge. After a few final arguments from Peter, the court denied his motion and took a brief recess. I had a few minutes to go and prep James as he awaited in the witness room. Before I could collect my case files, Peter walked over to my table.

"Remember young brother, it's never personal," quipped Peter.

I ignored him and hurried to the witness room to speak with James.

"Listen James, we are about to start the trial and you are our first witness," I said. "When you get on the stand, you have to keep your composure. This defense attorney is going to be very aggressive on cross-examination. He is going to do his best to piss you off. You have to stay calm and no matter what, don't become defensive or upset."

"I got you," replied James.

The clerk knocked on the door and informed us that the judge had taken the bench. I returned to the courtroom and introduced James as my first witness. On direct examination, he explained his story to the court as he had done with me and Officer Ivanov in the witness room. I knew Peter would crucify him if I painted him as a saint, so I asked questions about his past relationship with Tisha. He went into detail about their abusiveness towards one another and he admitted that the day he approached Tisha he was not happy to see her and his child walking with another man. I presented a simple theme: James stood a victim, albeit not one with clean hands. After I completed my direct, I turned to sit down and for the first time my eyes met with Tisha's. She looked terrified. As Peter started his cross-examination, I noticed that she didn't look at James as he spoke. She bowed her head with a childish deference.

Peter started his assault without hesitation. He sounded accusatory, his questions were argumentative, and he rarely let James finish his statements. As he asked questions, he paced back and forth around the courtroom like a bloodhound searching for its quarry. I would attempt to object to his line of questioning but Peter would talk louder over my objections and ignore them. Sometimes the judge would interject and ask me to repeat my objections and other times he would just let Peter continue without even addressing them. After a while, I sat down and gave up on many of objections; it was clear that Peter would persist, and the judge had begun to interject on his own out of frustration.

"James, you walked up behind them didn't you!" Peter said.

"Yes, I did," James replied.

"And you said, what's up!" Peter said again.

"Yes," said James.

"And you said it like, what's up! In a tone like you were ready to fight!" Peter suggested.

"No, I just said what's up, like what's going on," replied James.

"You were upset James! You weren't happy to see Tisha with her new boyfriend were you?!" Peter said.

"No, I--" replied James.

"Right?!" Said Peter.

"Objection your honor, the defense is not letting the witness finish his statement," I said.

"Mr. Robinson, could you please let the witness finish his statement and stop talking over the witness?" The judge requested angrily.

"Your honor, this is cross-examination. I have the right to confront this witness' version of the story," said Peter.

Peter continued this pattern on cross-examination for about two more minutes before the judge had seen and heard enough. He called us both to the bench, took his glasses off his face, and released his anger.

"Mr. Robinson, you will allow this witness to answer the question!" the judge screamed.

"But, your honor …" said Peter.

"I don't want to hear another word! If you say one more thing, I'll hold you in contempt of court. Do you hear me?"

I stood there silently in shock listening to the exchange. The judge ended the conversation at the bench and told Mr. Robinson to proceed. Mr. Robinson first returned to Tisha and she whispered some words in his ear.

"Your honor, my client has asked that I recuse myself from this trial after the exchange that she overheard at the bench. She does not believe that she can receive a fair trial in this case given the court's response to counsel."

"Your request is denied Mr. Robinson. Continue with your cross examination," the judge replied.

Mr. Robinson continued with his cross examination but tempered his questions and allowed James to answer them without cutting him off. James had taken Mr. Robinson's abuse better than I expected. Perhaps my pre-trial pep talk with him worked. He remained calm on the stand when Mr. Robinson pressed him about his prior history with Tisha.

Mr. Robinson's theory was that James was an abusive boyfriend who wanted to control Tisha, and seeing Tisha with another man around his child, infuriated him. James admitted to becoming upset but denied starting the altercation and maintained that it was Tisha who had started the fight. When James finished, I asked a few questions on redirect and after a few minutes he stepped down from the stand. I escorted him out of the courtroom and grabbed Tim from the witness room.

Tim took the stand and gave a similar story to the one he had given to police. He recalled sitting on top of the hill finishing his lunch when he heard James yelling to him from the base of the hill. When Tim went to investigate, he saw Tisha, and Eric surrounding James as he was attempting to walk away. Before Tim could get halfway down the hill, he saw Eric strike James on the side of the head and watched him fall to the ground. From there, all he could see was a scuffle on the ground. After the melee ended, Tim found himself just a few feet away from Tisha when she started walking towards James with the rock.

"Tim, did you see Tisha hit James with the rock?" I asked.

"No, I turned away and didn't see her actually strike James, but when I turned back his head was busted open," Tim responded.

I had never heard this version of the story. From the paperwork, it appeared that Tim had observed Tisha strike James with the rock. Peter immediately rose from his chair and asked to approach the bench.

"You honor, the government has committed a Brady violation in this case." yelled Peter. "This witness has testified inconsistent with the police paperwork. The government spoke with this witness about his story prior to him taking the stand, so they knew about this disparity and did not inform the defense in advance of trial."

"Your honor, this is the first time I am hearing this versions of events," I said sheepishly.

"I find that hard to believe your honor," retorted Peter.

Brady violations were a prosecutor's worst nightmare. Failing to provide the defense with evidence that tended to prove a defendant's innocence or lessen his or her punishment warranted sanctions by the court. Brady evidence ranged from failing to disclose an alibi witness to not informing the other side that one of your witnesses gave inconsistent statements. Intentional violations could cost an attorney his or her bar license.

160

Peter continued to press the issue. I attempted to conceal my nervousness; I couldn't recall Tim telling me he didn't see the blow and that is something I would have remembered, but in the haze of running around preparing for trial there was always a chance that I had missed something.

"I don't see any inconsistencies in his testimony. You may proceed counsel." explained the judge.

The tone of finality dissuaded Mr. Robinson from arguing further and I returned to questioning relieved that I hadn't been cited for a Brady violation. When I finished my direct, all I could think about was winning the trial. I had been accused of conducting a shoddy investigation, my witnesses were being humiliated on cross-examination and I had now been accused of a Brady violation. Peter was doing everything he could to derail my case. The battle had become personal to me; I was no longer fighting for the truth, I was fighting to win.

When Mr. Robinson completed his cross examination, we put on Officer Ivanov who was a brief fact witness. He explained his observations from his squad car. He too had not observed the strike but was involved in the arrest shortly after the assault. Peter drilled him on cross.

"Why would you leave a defenseless woman alone with a man she had just been assaulted by to follow another suspect?" said Peter.

Officer Ivanov hesitated.

"We thought the fight was over. We thought separating them was enough," said Ivanov.

Peter continued to deride Ivanov and his fellow officers on their poor police work for another thirty minutes before he finally finished his cross-examination. After two days of testimony, the government rested its case and it was time for Peter to put on his evidence.

Peter announced three witnesses for the defense. Eric was first; he stood 6'2 with a brawny physique. He was brown-skinned with a full beard and tattoos covered both his arms. When he took the stand, he slouched back in his chair prompting the judge to ask him to sit upright. Eric explained that he was dating Tisha for a few months and had accompanied her and her children to the bus stop. That day, they all planned to take the bus to a restaurant in Northwest D.C. Eric described James as being aggressive and disrespectful to the group.

"He came up to us pissed off, you know. He was cursing at Tisha and snatched Jeremiah away from Tisha's hands," said Eric.

"What did you do when he snatched Jeremiah away?" Peter asked.

"I told him to chill out, but then he started cursing at me," Eric responded.

"What happened after that?" said Peter.

"He started walking towards me and when he got in my face, I dropped him," Eric stated bluntly.

Eric went on to describe the scuffle on the ground and his exit once the police came. From my perspective, he was an innocent bystander caught in the middle of a domestic dispute, defending himself and Tisha from James' aggression. I cross-examined Eric and asked why he ran from the fight when the police came, especially if he cared so much about Tisha and had done nothing wrong.

"I was on probation man, I didn't want to go back to jail." He said emphatically.

I paused and retreated from my cross-examination. The response made sense and I had nothing else to ask Eric. Frankly, he wasn't an importance piece of the puzzle. He was not present when Tisha swung the rock, so realistically his involvement had nothing to do with the actual charge.

Next to the stand came Michael, Tisha's teenage son. This was my first time cross-examining a minor and I knew I needed to be strategic in my approach. Michael's age made him vulnerable to seemingly innocuous but insidious questions, but I didn't want to come across as manipulative to the judge. I also wanted to avoid Michael shutting down due to my aggressiveness. Midway through his story, I began to think differently about the case.

"Michael, tell us about the time James pulled a knife on your mom," Peter inquired.

"Your honor, what is the relevance of his this?" I asked.

"Your honor, the defendant is claiming self-defense in this case," responded Peter. "This prior incident goes to Tisha's state of mind when she swung the rock at James. We have to prove that she genuinely feared bodily harm."

"Overruled. You may continue young man," said the judge.

"James and my mom was fighting in the kitchen. I could hear them cursing at each other. I was in the other bedroom. My mom was upset because James had whooped me the other day and she didn't think he was right. They was pushing and shoving each other in the kitchen. Then James pulled out a knife and pointed it at my mom. She started crying and I started screaming for help."

"Was this the first time James had attacked your mom?" asked Peter.

"No, I saw him fight her a lot," said Michael.

Michael's story about the domestic abuse sounded genuine and unrehearsed. I looked into his eyes and saw the pain as he continued telling it. I glanced over at the defense table and saw that Tisha's eyes also began to swell with tears. Michael described several incidents between his mother and James. Each one resulting in various injuries to Tisha.

Michael discussed how James approached the group that day and grabbed his younger brother. Before he knew it, his mom fell to the ground struggling with James, so Michael jumped in to protect his mother. After the fight, he took his younger brother home.

"What happened when you took your brother home?" Peter continued.

"He had peed on himself and he was crying all the way home. When he got home he was still crying. When we got there, my aunt asked him what was wrong and I could hear him telling her what had happened," responded Michael.

"Objection your honor, hearsay," I intervened.

163

"Your honor, this is clearly an excited utterance. The child has urinated on himself and is crying about what happened," Peter replied.

"Your honor, this is several minutes after the event has occurred. The incident is over.

This is not an excited utterance." I said.

"I'll allow it," stated the judge.

Michael continued, "he said 'James hit mom.'"

This part of Michael's story seemed less convincing. I believed Tisha had planted this version of events in Michael's head and had coached him about what to say. It was too convenient that Michael couldn't remember other details of the incident but somehow he recalled in great detail the facts not only supporting an exciting utterance but also the specific conversation his brother had over six months ago with his aunt.

I quizzed him on the specific details of the scuffle, many of which were inconsistent with Eric's account. I also got him to admit his hatred for James, exposing his obvious bias against his former stepfather. I thought about asking him whether or not Tisha had coached him into telling the story about his little brother but, after a brief pause, I decided against it. I didn't want to force a young man to decide between disappointing his mother by telling the truth on the stand or lying and committing perjury. Plus, regardless if James started the fight on the hill, that didn't give Tisha the right to hit him with the rock. At least, this justification made me feel better going forward with the trial.

I began to realize that James probably was the aggressor on the hill that day. Even if he hadn't thrown the first blow, he certainly initiated the conflict by walking up to Tisha and threatening to take away Jeremiah. Although, in the eyes of the law, he hadn't committed a crime, James probably deserved every blow from a street justice perspective. He apparently had physically abused Tisha for years, at times taking his anger out on Michael when he could, yet he had never been convicted for any of his actions, because Tisha

164

either never called the police or never showed up in court, like many of my own victims.

Tisha finally took the stand and offered her version of events. She provided further details about the emotional and physical abuse she endured. I wondered if the physical abuse drove her to substance abuse and eventually homelessness. She was terrified of James.

The day of the incident, she wanted to spend some more time with Jeremiah before taking him home. Her phone had been cut off, so she couldn't contact James to let him know that she was going to keep him an extra day. Many aspects of her story didn't make sense. It was clear she was exaggerating much of what happened. She even described James as having a knife on him the day of the incident, a detail that neither Eric nor Michael ever mentioned. She testified that she believed that James would go for his knife and attack her.

Tisha described her fear on the park bench when all the officers left her alone with James just a few feet away. She picked up the net and rock in self-defense and stated that James approached her first. When James had come too close, she swung the rock out of self-defense.

The defense provided a camera phone video of Tisha recording herself moments before she struck James with the rock. The video offered mostly self-serving evidence of Tisha's fear of James—you could hear her pleading for help from God and pointing the camera towards James who stood several feet away. The video provided no evidence that James approached Tisha first.

After she testified, I had made up my mind that even though Tisha was guilty, she didn't really deserve a conviction. I didn't believe her story about James having a knife and approaching her first, but Tisha had endured enough abuse at the hands of James and, his condescending smile as she approached with the rock in hand, represented the last straw. He would not get the last laugh, not that day. I finished my cross-examination and Peter completed his redirect. We gave our closing arguments and the judge stated that she would take a day to decide the case.

Before I could leave the courtroom, Peter came up to me and pleaded that I speak with my supervisor about dismissing the case. I saw the defeat in his eyes. He knew Tisha hadn't come across as strong as he would have liked and his exchange with the judge only worsened his chances. We both knew the prospect of a conviction was high. I told him that I would think about it.

I was sitting in my office the next morning debating about what to do with the case when the felony supervisor gave me a call.

"Martinis, stop by when you get a chance, let's chat before you head to trial today," he asked.

How did he even know about my trial? I thought to myself.

A few minutes later I found myself in his office.

"Hey, you wanted me stop by?" I asked puzzled.

"Yeah, Peter Robinson called me yesterday about your case. He gave me the rundown and he says you've done a great job on the case so far. It looks like the defendant in this case is guilty but the history between the victim and the defendant appears to be a bit concerning. Is this really a case where justice will be served by convicting this woman? It seems like the guy got what he had coming."

Thinking about how Peter had gone behind my back and called my supervisor had me fuming inside. From my perspective, this reflected Peter's final attempt to sabotage my case. It immediately reminded me of all the tactics he had used throughout the trial to attack me.

"I think she's guilty," I said. "I agree that the victim doesn't have clean hands in this case but those things happened over two years ago and he suffered severe injuries. I think this is Peter Robinson's last attempt at getting his client off at all costs."

"Ok, look this is your case. I'm not going to make the decision for you. You know the case better than I do, so I'll let you make the decision whether or not to dismiss the case," he responded.

I walked out still irritated by Peter Robinson's sneak attack. I discussed the matter with a few of my colleagues. Many of them encouraged me to go with my gut and not to let our supervisor dissuade me from going forward with the case that I had worked so hard to prosecute.

The walk from my office to the courtroom went too quickly as I couldn't decide what to do. I wanted the case to go the distance; I had put in so many hours trying it. But I also empathized with Tisha. It was the sickest of ironies that the system would punish her and not James after all his abuses. I entered the courtroom a little late and saw that all the parties and the judge were waiting. As I approached the bench, I pondered whether I should dismiss the case.

"Mr. Jackson, does the prosecution have anything before the court renders its verdict in this case?" asked the judge.

Mr. Robinson looked at my table intently awaiting my response. I paused for ten seconds.

"No your honor. We are ready for the verdict." I said hesitantly.

Mr. Robinson dropped his head in disappointment. Tisha began to stare at the ceiling.

"On the count of possession of a prohibited weapon, the court finds the defendant guilty."

Tisha immediately burst out in tears and ran out of the courtroom. The judge asked the marshals to grab her and bring her back as Peter Robinson followed her and corralled her back to the defense table.

"On the count of simple assault, the court finds the defendant guilty." The judge stated.

Louder sobs rang from Tisha's face as Peter attempted to console her after the verdict. The judge allowed Tisha to go free until her sentencing date which was set a month out. The judge left the bench and I began packing my bags as Tisha stormed out of the courtroom crying. Peter collected his things and walked past my table. I noticed that his presence lingered and looked up to meet his eyes.

"Just remember young blood, it's never personal," he said.

In a matter of seconds, my decision impacted Tisha's life forever. I allowed my emotions and desire to win override my sense of justice. The mistake served as a grave irreversible one. Although I had done nothing wrong from a legal standpoint, I had done everything wrong from a moral one. I called James to inform him of the news.

"Good, I'm glad they convicted her. Where she headed now, central detention?" he said.

"No, she was released pending sentencing." I explained.

"Oh, aite. Cool. Appreciate it bro." He responded nonchalantly.

And that was it. I walked back to my office to a field of questions from colleagues wondering how the trial had gone. I explained that I had gotten a guilty verdict and many of them congratulated me. I offered a perfunctory response and closed the door to my office to reflect. Peter's words began to weigh on me like a crushing boulder. I had taken my job personally and my clouded judgment obscured the truth about Mr. Robinson's actions—he simply wanted to get the best results for his client. Was I becoming the type of prosecutor that I vowed never to become? It was at that moment that I realized the dangers of the profession—ego and competitiveness could be the most significant barriers to fairness in our criminal justice system. I could no longer be a part of it; it was changing me in ways that I knew I would regret.

PURPOSE

"Your purpose in life is to find your purpose
and give your whole heart and soul to it."

—GAUTAMA BUDDHA

After the end of the U.S. civil war, the psychologically wounded confederate stakeholders searched for ways to regain their political and economic power. Expectedly, southern whites were worried that the absence of cheap labor would significantly shake the distribution of wealth in the south, at minimum making the agricultural based economy less profitable and at worse sending many of them into poverty. Conversely, the abolishment of forced labor appeared to offer an unprecedented opportunity for African Americans to enter the field of politics and participate in the economy while, for the first time, benefiting from the fruits of their labor.

Unfortunately for pro-egalitarians, political differences, violence and terrorism destroyed the initiatives of those who supported full integration of African Americans into society. Supporters of the status quo relied in part on fear to preserve their political and economic power over African Americans. Terrorist groups such as the Ku Klux Klan emerged, killing and intimidating blacks and whites who sought to disrupt their political agendas. White supremacist organizations like the Klan however could not have existed without the support of a complicit criminal justice system, a system which has historically served as an accomplice to pervasive civil rights violations. Law enforcement endorsed racism by engineering false charges against African Americans and ignoring legitimate crimes committed by whites. The judges, prosecutors and defense attorneys shared responsibility. Judges ignored defendant's constitutional rights. Prosecutors often ignored or withheld evidence. Defense attorneys encouraged plea deals for the innocent.

During this "Jim Crow" era, Washington, D.C. not only served as the nation's capital—a nation that purported to be the leader of the free world—but also remained a region where racial inequality and systemic racism was deeply woven into the fabric of the social, economic and legal infrastructure of the city. Despite D.C. becoming the first major U.S. city with a majority black population, its arbitrary label as a federal territory stripped African Americans of the opportunity to control the political landscape and harness the power that their majority title held. Ironically, disgruntled Southern Whites in Congress controlled D.C.'s local politics. As a result, laws that supported racial segregation prevailed and created negative implications for African Americans who were discriminated against in housing, employment, and just about every other aspect of daily life that one can imagine. African Americans were denied access to mortgages; those who wanted to purchase homes with cash were refused by owners whose deeds contained restrictive covenants. The public schools to which African Americans were relegated lacked sufficient funding from elementary all the way up to post-secondary education, guaranteeing that blacks would receive subpar education. It was common practice to discriminate against blacks in employment and pay, despite reconstruction laws that prohibited the widespread custom.

Although the integration of schools across the country marked the end of segregation and Jim Crow laws, African Americans continued to suffer from widespread social inequalities. Poverty pervaded black communities as did the threat of violence from hate groups and local militarized police forces. At the same time, the non-violent approach of the civil rights movement was giving way to a more revolutionary response to racial injustice. Groups such as the Black Panther Party for self-defense began to emerge as an armed response to the civil rights struggle and nowhere did these groups find stronger opposition than the nation's capital. The city served as headquarters to the FBI, an agency then run by J. Edgar Hoover, who created a unit dedicated to dismantling black-led domestic organizations that sought to fight systemic racism, promote education, and encourage black unity. The agency is often cited for cooperating with local police and identifying certain black leaders as targets for smear campaigns, false criminal charges, and even assassinations.

During the war initiated by the U.S. government against domestic organizations, a new system emerged. Those who sought a new way to maintain the status quo of social and economic control realized that criminalization was a much more insidious and effective means of perpetuating social inequality. Suddenly, the government declared a war on drugs before a drug problem even existed in the U.S. Shortly thereafter, drugs smuggled from South America hit the U.S. by the tons and were dumped into poor communities – the "ghettos" that were created by the very people who labeled them as such. Later, evidence surfaced that the concentration of drugs in African American and other minority communities was no coincidence but rather an epidemic that the U.S. government was aware of and did nothing to stop.

It should come as no surprise that the nation's largest majority black city was hit the hardest by crack cocaine, turning the territory into the "nation's murder capital" in the early 1990s. The war on drugs in D.C. and across the country became a political platform for politicians looking to score points with voters who viewed the drug problem as a black problem that confirmed racist stereotypes: blacks were "super predators" who belonged in prison. The battle offered politicians a perfect opportunity to shift the focus from the still existing system of racism that locked African Americans out of equal opportunities to the uptick in violence and drug use engineered by the same government that was now ostensibly fighting against it. Thousands of African-American families were destroyed by prison sentences, drug addiction, and violent crimes.

Fast forward a few decades, there I was prosecuting crimes in the city formerly known as Chocolate City. A city that was starting to look more Neapolitan than Rocky Road as suburban white flight returned to gentrify the city. Crime rates had fallen precipitously, the city had seen its first black president, and D.C.'s growing black middle class became one of the wealthiest and most educated concentration of African Americans in the country. Still, there was at least one place you could visit to witness the lasting impact that systemic racism had created on the city. It was a place I visited every day of the week as a prosecutor: the local criminal courthouse. Ninety-nine percent of the defendants I prosecuted were African American men. When I read their pre-sentencing reports, I noticed a clear pattern of childhood and adult experiences: 1) poverty, 2) broken families, and 3) drug abuse. I knew that many of these factors were a direct result of the past and present system. At times, I could not help but reflect upon the two systems that African Americans encountered in America: 1) the insidious and less visible system of discrimination perpetrated primarily by ignorance and apathy, and 2) the visible criminal justice system—of which I had become a participant.

One night while riding the metro home from work, I noticed a young African American man sitting across from me on the train. He appeared about twenty years old with shoulder length dreadlocks sprouting from his head. He wore a black hoodie with camouflage pants, Nike Foamposite sneakers and earbuds blaring in his ears. The near empty train held a few other passengers sprawled out on the other side of the car. I watched in the corner of my eye as the young man continued rocking back and forth to the beat. I was carrying a backpack with nothing of value inside except my car keys. After a few stops, the young man moved closer to my seat heading towards the double doors to exit. As he approached, I secured my backpack in front of me by positioning it between my legs to make it more difficult to grab. The young man hadn't even noticed my action. He stepped off the metro and hugged a young woman and a young girl waiting for him on the platform. I watched him embrace the two—the three of them walked away as my train accelerated into the tunnel.

Feelings of guilt and questions about the impact of my time as a prosecutor tormented me on the ride home. Many of my defendants looked like that young man standing on the train and yet so did many of my own family members and friends. I recalled my first months as a prosecutor and how I could recall the faces of each of my defendants. However, as time went on, I barely looked in their direction during hearings or in passing in the courthouse. All I needed to know was their name and their charges. I had become desensitized to the daily incarceration of black faces. Witnessing droves of young black men in chains became normal and expected. In fact, seeing any other race in an orange jumpsuit was a rare occasion that invoked questions of "I wonder what he did?" and "what's he in here for?" Despite understanding the historical context that created the racial disparities in the criminal justice system, I found it hard to combat the psychological impact of the daily exposure to black people who were accused and convicted of horrific offenses. That impact manifested itself on the train that day when I misjudged that young man for no other reason than his appearance.

I knew I had arrived at a crossroad in my prosecutorial career. On one hand, I had finally established a system for balancing the scales of justice on my own terms. Although I knew my contributions would not transform the system overnight, I believed in the importance of bringing about change on all levels no matter how small. On the flip side, the very system that I despised and hoped to rectify was gradually creating within me an implicit bias that I was embarrassed to admit existed. Could I continue to convince myself that the modest differences I made outweighed the reality that I would continue to observe an assembly line of black faces ushered through the criminal justice system? Did I possess the willpower to fight and win my own internal battle against indoctrination?

The Last Straw

It was January 20, 2017 around 11:00 p.m. I was sitting in the courtroom awaiting the court to present the last group of prisoners. That day, I had arraigned over two hundred defendants in a span of ten hours and I was finally about to end what had been an extremely taxing Saturday. The previous day, Justice Clarence Thomas swore in Donald Trump as the country's 45th president at his dubiously, self-proclaimed record setting inauguration. That same day, right around the corner from the White House, dozens of protesters had taken to the streets in opposition to Trump's presidency sparking the first major riot in the nation's capital since Martin Luther King's assassination in 1968.

That week, I was still in shock from the election results and brooding over the thought of working for a Justice Department run by Jeff Sessions and Donald Trump, two men who represented a reversion to the days of overt oppression and racial hostility. I signed up for the Saturday arraignment scheduled months in advance and I knew about the riots from the previous day. I expected a long day in court but significantly underestimated how draining the experience would be. The marshals were bringing the suspected rioters out in groups of ten. All of them chained from hand to feet standing side-by-side. Almost all of them comprised white men and women in their early twenties. Spectators filled the courtroom, observing the proceedings and awaiting the release of their loved ones. I was the only U.S. attorney in the courtroom. There were only a few arraignments for the local prosecutor representing the District's Office of Attorney General and those cases were called early in the afternoon allowing him to avoid sitting through ten hours of arraignments. Once he finished, he collected his files and flashed a sympathetic salute in my direction before hustling out of the building to meet a bevy of local news reporters.

When the marshals funneled groups of young men and women out from the back, I stood up and prepared to give my short, rehearsed speech to the court. Our office was not requesting the court detain any of the suspects, which made my job much more manageable. No detention request meant no need to argue probable cause. The hearings in theory should have taken no longer than a few minutes for each defendant. Unfortunately, theory and practice were not aligned. The absence of a need to argue didn't mean the defense attorneys refrained from doing so. Quite the contrary, many of them relished in the opportunity to perform in front of a massive congregation.

I noticed the presence of a particularly annoying defense attorney standing next to one of the accused rioters. It was one of the public defender services' more notorious members. I once had a detention hearing—hearings which usually lasted 15-30 minutes— go on for two hours because of his courtroom antics. His infamy stemmed from 1) a penchant for constructing fishy legal arguments and 2) an untrustworthy approach to criminal defense work. In another shared case between us, we negotiated a plea agreement well in advance of the hearing which included a specific agreed upon sentence for the defendant. I could not attend the hearing and requested that one of my colleagues handle the sentencing. During the hearing, the defense attorney took advantage of my colleague's lack of knowledge about the case and advocated for a different sentence that the judge accepted.

When I saw this attorney standing up waiting to address the court, I expected a show and he certainly delivered.

"And how does the defendant respond to these charges?" asked the court.

"Your honor, my client requests immediate dismissal and release from this case. The government has saw fit to charge two hundred people in direct violation of their 1st amendment Constitutional right to protest the election of Donald Trump as president. I ask that the court recuse Mr. Jackson as prosecutor in this case."

The judge looked up from the document in front of her and smirked. "And why is that counsel?"

"He is not impartial in this matter. His boss is Donald Trump; the very person that my clients were protesting yesterday afternoon. In fact, I demand that this court recuse every U.S. Attorneys' office in the country from this case as there is nowhere in the country my client can receive a fair trial while Donald Trump is president. The prosecutor should be ashamed of himself for representing a government that indiscriminately rounds up hundreds of innocent citizens on trumped up charges—no pun intended—for doing nothing illegal at all."

The entire crowd cheered in unison including the ten men and women shackled behind their lawyers. The judge shouted for order in the court and the yells quickly turned to murmurs. My face turned red with embarrassment and anger. I knew the arguments held little weight from a legal standpoint but that didn't matter to me. I wanted to fire back with a witty response and defend my integrity. I wanted to tell everyone in the courtroom that they were more likely to find me among the arrested than a group of Trump supporters. I wanted to explain to the protestors that my hands were tied and that if I had the power to dismiss their cases I would. But I couldn't.

"Your honor, the government has no objection to releasing the defendants on their own personal recognizance," I stated.

I endured five hours of similar attacks from different attorneys and offered the same line as my only response. When the night ended, I reflected on my time as a prosecutor and decided that it had come to an end. The system needed me, and others who shared my views, now more than ever but I could no longer participate in the process. My conscious would not let me. This is not to say that my former colleagues who remain prosecutors today are somehow inherently depraved or ignorant of the flaws in the system. Many of them are honorable men and women who have committed their lives to reforming the structure from within. I admired them and understood the importance of that undertaking, but, for me, the confluence of feelings of helplessness, anger, and ambivalence served as sufficient burden and the election of an incompetent and racist president represented the final straw.

My time as a prosecutor had ended but I would never forget the countless lives I impacted during my tenure. I created life-long friendships with my fellow prosecutors and I discovered a new-found respect for the profession. However, I knew that I would never reach my purpose in life of spiritual fulfillment by serving in this capacity as an agent of the state.

62033906R00112

Made in the USA
Columbia, SC
28 June 2019